COMMON ¢ENT$

ECONOMICS+POLITICS+FINANCE

A CITIZEN'S
SURVIVAL
GUIDE

by
MICHAEL HARRINGTON, MBA, PhD

"Change is inevitable. Change is constant."
— *Benjamin Disraeli*

"It is not the strongest of the species that survive, nor the most intelligent, but the one most responsive to change."
— *Charles Darwin*

[THIS PAGE INTENTIONALLY LEFT BLANK]

CONTENTS

Acknowledgments i

Author's Note iii

Executive Summary ix

Introduction xi

Chapter One - A Simple Model 1
    1.1 Let's Eat! Now or Later?* 2
    1.2 I Like What You Have - Let's Trade* 3
    1.3 I Need Some $Money$** 3
    1.4 Debt and Credit** 4
    1.5 Capital vs. Labor: Friends or Foes?** 7
    1.6 Risk, Return and Uncertainty** 10

Chapter Two - The Macroeconomy 14
    2.1 Market Failures** 16
    2.2 The Mystique of Money*** 18
    2.3 Financial Alchemy*** 21
    2.4 Capital and Financial Markets*** 24
    2.5 Labor and the Problem of Unemployment** 28
    2.6 Competing Macroeconomic Theories** 29
    2.7 Distributional Failures* 32
    2.8 Globalization: National vs. International Economy** 33
    2.9 Risk, Uncertainty, and Insurance** 36

Chapter Three -The Politics of Policy 42
    3.1 Democracy and the Two-Party System* 43
    3.2 Federalism* 45
    3.3 Politics and Policy* 46
    3.4 The Media* 47
    3.5 Red vs. Blue?* 48
    3.6 Elites, Oligarchies, and Plutocracies* 50

Chapter Four - Applying the Model to Policy 53
    4.1 The Great Moderation, The Credit Bubble and Financial Crises** 53
        4.1.1 A House is Not Just a Home?* 57
    4.2 The Policy Agenda 62
        4.2.1 Private and Social Insurance** 67
        4.2.2 Distributional Issues** 70
        4.2.3 Capitalism For All** 71

Chapter Five - The Main Policy Challenges 74
    5.1 Federal Reserve Policy*** 74

5.2 Fiscal Reform** 80

5.3 Tax Reform** 81

5.4 Risk, Insurance, and Entitlements** 87

5.5 The Principal-Agent Problem** 89

Conclusion 96

    The Curse of the Market** 100

Appendix A -A Gross Over-Simplification of Economics*** 108

Appendix B - What's Wrong with Economics?*** 112

Appendix C - The Credit-Debt Machine*** 114

About the Author 118

Reading List 119

Glossary 121

Notes 130

Difficulty Factor:
    * = easy
    ** = moderate
    *** = challenging

ACKNOWLEDGMENTS

I would like to express my gratitude for those who have helped add invaluable clarity and comprehension to this presentation. Without such generous assistance I'm sure the ideas expressed here would be understood fully by the author alone, if I may be so presumptuous. The list will grow as the book circulates, but I will mention here David Magee, Jon Fitzsimmons, and Todd Mittleman. I've had many fine teachers in economics, finance, political science, and public policy. I will spare them unsolicited publicity, but no blame can be laid at their feet.

As always, my inestimable gratitude is reserved for my wife, unpaid editor, and best friend, Tushara Bindu Gude, who, as an art historian, labored over these pages to make sense of, and correct, my convoluted thoughts. I dedicate this book to her and hope she is never embarrassed for it. All errors are mine alone.

[THIS PAGE INTENTIONALLY LEFT BLANK]

AUTHOR'S NOTE

Economics is the fine art of managing change through exchange.

There is an ancient Chinese proverb that says, "May you live in interesting times." (Some may consider this as more of a curse.) The past few years certainly have proven interesting for those of us who study politics and economics, but perhaps have been less appreciated by others who have lived through them. My training is in political science, finance, and economics. I practice my trade through writing, researching, and policy analysis. Since the beginning of this episode we now refer to as The Great Recession (which is probably not really over yet), I've encountered endless questions in casual social gatherings: What happened? What is going to happen now? How did this happen? Who's to blame? Is our politics broken? What can be done? How do I protect myself? Come on, aren't you a political scientist and economist?!

Each time, I have to humbly confess that I don't have the answers and mumble something about how "it depends." (Economists are great at faking humility.) But, of course, this is not really very helpful. So, I follow up with: "Well, that is a *big* question." The faint of heart then turn the conversation back to sports, or to the subtleties of a delicate pinot noir.

Okay, not always. For those who persist, I feel compelled to frame these open-ended questions within the larger context of our society and how to understand it. Such attempts are the least we can do as social scientists; non-economists should be engaged in more pleasant activities than wondering what the so-called experts are chatting about. I also believe that the essence of politics and economics can be reduced, essentially, to simple intuition and common sense of the Mark Twain variety. Although the subject of high finance gets more esoteric and it helps to have experience in the field, for the most part our experts have only succeeded in making a complex world even more incomprehensible. Unfortunately, journalists and politicians have often valiantly waded in to explain this world but get their explanations mostly wrong, while sprinkling their politics and ideological opinions into the mix. I have often wished I could point the intellectually curious to a simple exposition of our modern political economy—one that could be easily consumed, with a minimum of indigestion. Thus came the idea to offer *A Citizen's Survival Guide*.

I argue that a more comprehensive understanding of our political economy, our economic institutions, and the policies we enact is of the utmost importance to the average citizen today. Momentous changes are unfolding within our world. These changes, coming at an increasing pace, will affect each and every one of us in the years to come. The chosen cure for the financial crisis of 2008, for instance, has been to transfer wealth from savers and taxpayers to banks and other creditors in order to shore up an insolvent banking system. The zero interest rates on current savings accounts are no accident – they are a result of a deliberate policy to re-inflate asset prices (i.e. stocks, bonds and real estate), in order to save the value of collateral on non-performing loans that threaten the financial system. The same banks that are receiving no-interest loans from the Federal Reserve are turning around and buying Treasury bonds at 3% risk-free returns. In plain speak, the Fed is lending banking conglomerates free money so that the government (us!) can then borrow it back from them at 3%! These banks then use the profits to pay out large bonuses and rebuild the capital they lost from the bad loans they made. More alarming, this public-private credit system is also funding government deficit spending at an exploding rate.[1] These are *our* debts and one wonders when the voters were consulted. Let us put this another way: There is a large entity in the economy that is motivated to create and extend credit (the banking system backed by the Federal Reserve) and an even larger entity interested in borrowing and issuing debt (the government). It just so happens that this symbiotic credit-debt relationship is entirely underwritten and paid for by the US taxpayer.[2] How many of us get to play "heads we win, tails you lose" on a scale of this magnitude?

A conspiracy theorist might conclude this is all a nefarious plot for political and financial elites to accumulate vast amounts of national wealth without ever being held to account by the people who pay. Conspiracy or not, this is a great system if you can keep it under wraps so depositors, taxpayers, and citizens are unaware of what's really going on.

The Fed's aforementioned reflation policy is trumpeted by the media and by politicians who claim it is "keeping people in their homes." But who really wants to keep paying for an overpriced home over the next 20-30 years? Those kinds of investments will make homeowners destitute, not financially secure. In the meantime, people who are prudently saving and living within their means (many of them elderly and on fixed incomes) are paying dearly in foregone interest and higher energy and food prices. Such policies will continue until voter-taxpayers understand and assert their interests at the voting booth without being distracted by the latest scare tactics and white noise generated, usually with a heavy dose of ignorance, by our two political parties.

Access to health care and the security of retirement pensions are two more critical challenges for our current politics. Both issues relate to an important concept addressed in this guide—the gradual shifting of risk in our free society. This trend has fomented growing political tensions over whether governments can provide for the social welfare needs of their citizens, or whether they even need to. Our changing economy is affecting our jobs, careers, incomes, families, wealth, safety, and our society's future stability and well-being. Similar changes are occurring across the globe, whether we like it or not. Our institutions and policies need to empower us to adapt easily to change. We can argue over the costs and benefits of globalization and fight battles over political ideology, but this all seems beside the point. As a former teacher of political economy, I have found that economics and politics are too malleable and complex to understand clearly from a purely ideological position. One needs an open mind to challenge the conventional wisdom that bombards us from both ends of the political spectrum.

In full disclosure, I will admit that my own preferences are aligned with those principles articulated in America's Declaration of Independence, that *we are endowed…with certain unalienable Rights, that among these are Life, Liberty and the pursuit of Happiness.* These principles translate into an explicit preference for functioning political democracy and economic freedom, both of which obtain in an open, competitive environment characterized by 1) free markets for economic exchange, and 2) participatory political democracy. These provide the core of political liberalism in the historical sense; they are embraced by classical liberalism on the conservative or libertarian 'right,' as well as by democratic liberalism espoused on the populist 'left.' I will assert that the ideas I present in this guide can be embraced regardless of ideological faith. Not only do I advocate for free markets, but also for a strong safety-net to protect citizens from vicissitudes of the economy beyond their control. Many of our public debates degenerate into these arguments over free markets, social welfare, and true democracy, but if we believe in the form of political *liberalism* on which the United States of America was founded, the question we should ask is not whether we have achieved these conditions in perfection, but whether economic and political freedoms provide a useful lodestar to guide our actions and aspirations. I believe they do. My recommendation is to put partisan political ideology aside—it is not helpful to intellectual objectivity. That's all I believe I need to say on the matter.

This is not an economics text or a thorough critique of recent events – others have offered these in abundance. For the sake of brevity, I will not treat economic issues comprehensively, but will try to provide a practical overview so readers may better understand the "big picture." My appeal is to intuition. I offer here a conceptual approach to economics and politics that does not require technical training, but is nevertheless sufficient to help one make informed judgments about policy choices. It serves in some ways as a citizen or voter's guide, hence the title. In a free society, voting and making our opinions known to political representatives is the most direct way to influence policy choices that affect us all.

There are two main threads that orient the presentation. First and foremost, is a focus on fundamental *economics*. For generations, students were told that economics is the study of supply and demand. Yes, supply is what we produce and demand is what we consume, and where they meet is the equilibrium price that insures we produce all we consume and vice-versa. Economics is also characterized as the science of making trade-offs in a world of scarce and finite resources. Both of these definitions are useful to our understanding of the workings of economics, but I offer another, more prosaic, addendum to that definition: *Economics is the fine art of managing change through exchange.*

Supply, demand, and budget trade-offs are often studied through static economic analysis, while the world we live in is dynamic. Static analysis is like a photograph that captures a single moment in time. We can draw supply and demand curves on a graph and see the immediate relationships and measure their magnitude. Dynamic analysis is like a movie with scenes, characters, and plots that constantly change. We must follow the story through time in order to fully understand it. Our world is constantly changing and this change is a fundamental concept of macroeconomics.

By nature, all living organisms must adapt to change in order to survive. In adapting to survive, humans have learned to work together, much like other social animals. We've banded together in communities and developed a highly differentiated division of labor. We use exchange markets to efficiently manage our risks while maximizing our welfare. In so doing, we are forced to make choices from among an almost infinite array of options: Should I go to medical school or law school? Should I become a banker or an actor? Should I buy a house or rent? Live in New York or Oklahoma? Buy a Prius or a Porsche? Should I marry this person or that? Do it now or later? Many of these choices are constrained because they are either mutually exclusive or they exceed the limits of our budgets. So we prioritize, weigh the trade-offs, and commit to our fates. We cannot avoid facing such choices: if we want economic security in old age, there are actions we will all need to take before we get there. The strategy is fairly straightforward: we continually advance toward our life objectives while staying flexible in case outside events force us to change our path.

When we add up these choices, trade-offs, and exchanges among millions of individuals we have the essential makings of a market economy. As we study and analyze these activities we can develop a framework for understanding how everything does, or doesn't, work. The best our economic theories can do is to make sure we are making the right choices given our goals. I hope the essence of this process can be described most simply as that *fine art of managing change through exchange.*

The second thread that runs through this guide is its focus on actual policies and their outcomes, an analysis that encompasses economics, finance, and politics. Our policy discussions will rely on both a theoretical understanding based on applied economics, and an empirical approach that attempts to evaluate recent events. The Great Recession is primarily a financial phenomenon that severely impacted the real economy and the political arena, so we will apply our economic thinking in a practical sense to these various problems that challenge us.

I use a simple visual concept to help orient the "big picture" relationship between economics and politics. Economics is like a box with rigid sides that act as constraints. Politics is our latitude to make different social choices as long as they respect the boundary constraints of the box. In other words, politics will determine how we allocate resources in society, but economics will determine how many or few resources we will have to distribute. Our policies should seek to loosen our economic constraints by expanding the sides of the box so we have more resources with which to achieve our social goals.

For this guide to be effective it should be short, simple and, I hope, perfectly comprehensible to the average high school student. The rudimentary approach is deliberate; one must understand how to carve a block of stone in all its dimensions and qualities before one builds a cathedral. And we must be familiar with the conventional before we can explore the unconventional. Thus, my chosen methods may appear overly simplistic at times, but the purpose is to challenge the logic of a very complex edifice. Understanding macroeconomic relationships requires a certain concentration of mind and careful study. As much as I would like, I cannot spoon-feed *all* the relevant knowledge in a guide so brief, so I confess this simplified guide will still challenge the thoughtful mind (it's longer than I had hoped and still grows like kudzu). I have attached asterisks to different sections of the guide to indicate the difficulty factor. Like a hot meter on an Indian or Mexican food menu, * designates the material as easy, ** as moderate, and *** as challenging.

I will not be introducing lots of statistics, graphs, or mathematical concepts, as I believe these can overly complicate the fundamental understanding of political economy and scare off the mathematically timid. Such data and formulations are easily discovered on the Internet these days and I provide links where appropriate. In order to keep the narrative flowing, many terms and arcane concepts (underlined) are explained with expanded footnotes and references in the glossary.

My purpose is to appeal to reason, common sense, and logic, not to scholarly erudition. Many seemingly obvious issues will be investigated at more profound levels of meaning that trained economists often take for granted (and sometimes get wrong). For example: What is capital? What is money? What determines the value of money? How is wealth produced? How is it distributed? Why do we have business cycles? How can hedge funds make billions of dollars and yet produce nothing? And what the heck is QE2 if not a cruise ship?

Please be advised that what you read here is the beginning of a public and personal journey, hopefully down the right road to your desired destination.

EXECUTIVE SUMMARY

- **Time, uncertainty, and risk**: Our physical and social worlds pass through time, introducing change, uncertainty, and risk. These are the concepts that inform our study of economics, finance, and politics.

- **Consumption/acquisitiveness** is the traditional foundation of classical economic theory. However, we need to incorporate **uncertainty** into our contextual framework and **loss aversion** into our behavioral assumptions in order to comprehend macro phenomena.

- **Loss aversion** is at the root of political demands for **social insurance entitlements** and government intervention into the economy.

- **Sustainable growth is the primary objective of economic policy.** Long-term **labor productivity** and **capital accumulation** are the sources of real wealth.

- Sustainability and stability through time is a function of individual and systemic **adaptability to change**.

- The input/output flows of the economy are **distributional problems** that need to balance consumption, production, and investment through time.

- **Monetary phenomena cannot substitute for real phenomena**. The role of the term structure of **interest rates** is crucial to managing the balance required for long-term market stability and economic sustainability.

- **Financial markets are inherently unstable** because asset price movements promote herd behavior. This herd behavior becomes more threatening to the system with **excessive debt and credit financing** relative to equity.

- The main **policy challenges** we face are:

    1. **Transparent Federal Reserve policy** that targets the stable value of the currency and the financial integrity of the banking system.
    2. **Entitlement reform** to manage risk through a combination of self-insurance, private insurance markets, and social insurance, in that order of priority.
    3. **Tax reform** that balances budgetary requirements across different sources of tax revenue by function: consumption, production, and wealth. Tax policy should align with economic growth through private capital accumulation and productivity.
    4. **Agency failures** in all institutional settings must be managed with transparency, open competition, and accountability, combined with regulatory statutes and oversight.
    5. **Skewed distributions** of resources, especially income and financial wealth that can best be mitigated by understanding the mechanisms of the market and the interaction with policy.
    6. **A more responsive democratic political process** by controlling the agency problems in government through electoral competition, transparency, and accountability.

INTRODUCTION

I have subtitled this book deliberately as a guide to the economy, but with the essential roles of politics and financial markets integrated to show how these specific spheres of our modern world interact to shape the whole. This approach is a deliberate return to past traditions of scholarship. Before the early to mid-20th century, intellectuals who studied the social sciences called themselves political economists or historians. Adam Smith, David Ricardo, Karl Marx, Joseph Schumpeter, Friedrich Hayek, and John Maynard Keynes all studied the world in an integral manner. It was only when social science progressed technically and became highly specialized that we divided its various disciplines into separate schools of knowledge. We pay a price for the efficiency gains of specialization when we crowd out comprehensive knowledge. By the late 20th century, when I was studying at the academy, the common joke was that a sociologist was a failed historian, a historian a failed political scientist, a political scientist a failed economist, an economist a failed mathematician, and a mathematician a failed physicist. The progression leads towards more and more technically complex disciplines, suggesting if one isn't smart enough to study physics, perhaps a step back to sociology is a more viable career choice. (Apologies here to sociologists – it's only a joke.) To complete this circle to its logical conclusion, a physicist is merely a failed philosopher, wherein technical proficiency has reached its final disutility in understanding the meaning of existence.

I started my career in economics in the 1970s. The profession has changed drastically in the past forty years, becoming more and more focused on mathematical precision. (I confess I have not kept pace with the math.) But the world we study has also changed in important ways. With the breakdown in the early 1970s of the Bretton Woods system that governed international trade relations and currency exchange, the sheer volume of trade in international capital and foreign exchange markets has exploded, dwarfing the real goods markets.[3] This expansion of international finance has been facilitated by the revolution in information and communications. The result is that the tail of finance is wagging the dog of international trade and commerce. Finance theory and the study of international capital markets have become critical to understanding macroeconomics and to formulating policy. Today, no economist can understand the capitalist world economy without a solid grounding in finance and capital markets.

To compound our difficulties, the political evolution of democracy and freedom has led to more transparency and greater participation in electoral politics and policymaking. So, while the international economy has become more closely linked with international capital flows, the role of national and international politics has exerted greater influence in determining policy choices and outcomes. This is a good thing, but through this democratization we have learned how futile economic theorizing can be without factoring in the political process.

We also have the difficulty of predicting human behavior, which is the most basic building block in the study of the social sciences. The complex mathematical models of macroeconomic analysis are based on simplistic and convenient assumptions about behavior that do not necessarily hold under real world conditions. Consequently, these models' veracity has become highly suspect (more on this shortly). The sad tale of our recent financial debacle shows that many of our top economists do not understand how financial markets work, our political leaders and government regulators do not understand economics, and most scary of all, our financial experts in the banking industry do not seem to understand their own mathematical risk models!

There is another joke often repeated in intellectual circles: a *specialist* studies a subject in such focus and depth that soon he or she come to know *everything about nothing*, while a *generalist* is so overwhelmed by the breadth of knowledge that soon he or she ends up knowing *nothing about everything*. We need a good balance between these two extremes. Unfortunately, we have far too few deep, well-balanced generalists. One, because the sheer volume of knowledge they must integrate is immense, and two, because our market society overwhelmingly favors the division of labor and rewards the expert/specialist. This is apparent in both the university and the marketplace. We suffer the consequences most deeply at the pinnacle of leadership. Our recent leadership failures suggest that comprehensive policymaking belongs to the realm of the wise and experienced multi-disciplined generalist, not to the specialist.

Another point I would like to reiterate in this introduction is that economics and its related disciplines are founded on simple common sense. The esoteric jargon bantered about is sometimes necessary for preciseness of meaning and shorthand communication between professionals, but beneath the big words and theories lie the most rudimentary and intuitively obvious concepts. (Jargon makes experts feel and sound more important, to justify the high fees they hope to earn for their musings.) Sweep away the jargon and these basic, intuitive, economic concepts lend themselves to a variety of more concrete analogies and metaphors. If you suspect wealth is really created by hard work, saving, and prudent investing, rather than by the interest rate manipulations of the Federal Reserve, you're on the right track. (Perhaps we should send a few copies of *Poor Richard's Almanac* to Washington?)

A final point: in addition to finance and economics, I will offer a brief overview of democratic politics, specifically American politics. I have been researching presidential voting patterns—and that ubiquitous red-blue political divide—since 2000. The misperceptions perpetuated across the land regarding such divisions have become an impediment to our democratic governing process. If we can't govern as a pluralistic democracy of diverse and varied groups, then this talk about policy becomes superfluous and we will deserve what we end up with. Most ordinary people understand this intuitively and reject the rank partisanship that divides our politics. But politics is emotional and sometimes we lose our grip on reason, which is why our grandmothers told us to avoid discussing politics (and religion) altogether in polite social circles. However, we can take heart. The scientist in me knows that we have ways of testing beliefs empirically and this factual evidence can and must be weighed against pure faith-based ideology.

By the end of this guide I hope to have framed some of the most pressing political and economic issues that confound our society. We need to understand our recent financial meltdown in its historical context, which goes back at least two generations. We need to understand our future in terms of government entitlement programs and clearly define the public vs. private sphere of responsibility. We need to be able to understand the trade-offs between taxing and spending and how to sustain the stable improvement in our standard of living and quality of life. We need to understand how to order our society so that we can achieve the lives we choose and also preserve our freedoms. We must pay careful attention to such issues as education, healthcare, old age insurance, inequality, and the environment. But first we must have a framework of understanding to help us make the decisions that will best address these many challenges.

The complexity of our society often appears like a gigantic jigsaw puzzle, its pieces strewn about on the ground. Our task is to put the pieces of the puzzle in their proper place in order to see the big picture and the complete solution. There's nothing a jigsaw puzzle demands more than patience and persistence.

I will present a foundation of simple related concepts upon which we can build a model that simplifies our tasks. Economists love models (the kinds of models architects use to design buildings, not the ones we fantasize about during a Victoria's Secret television special). Models are mental constructs that help us focus on, and manipulate, the most fundamental pieces of the puzzle, so that we are not distracted by thousands of less important elements. Think of how we solve a jigsaw puzzle—we look for edge pieces to frame out the puzzle and then group together similar color shades such as sky or water. Then we try to find the pieces that link these larger elements together, the whole time using the completed picture on the cover box to guide us.

Models are constructed of building blocks, one laid upon the other until the edifice we previously conceived only in our imaginations is realized in full.

There are two basic building blocks on which our analysis rests, and which I cannot emphasize enough. The first is the idea that all economic decisions can be reduced to *the simple choice of whether to consume now or at some future time.* This will be explained more fully in the next chapter. We'll see that this is the most fundamental economic choice we must make each day. It drives everything else in economic analysis. When we discuss issues like interest rates, or saving, or investing or producing, the analysis can be reduced to how it affects that simple decision to consume now or later.

The second building block relates to the most basic human instinct that influences our choices and preferences. This instinct has often been referred to as risk aversion, but is more accurately defined as *loss aversion.* Loss aversion flows from a survival instinct that makes us most sensitive to perceptions of risk. Behavioral studies and experiments have shown how human subjects are much more conscious of threats of loss than they are to possible gains.[4] This has profound implications for how we respond to a changing world. As you proceed through the economic analyses that follow, keep in mind these two behavioral foundations of our model: *consume now or later* and *avoid loss.*

In the following chapter we will construct a simple economic model. Once we have this as a solid reference point, we will then add some complexity to it, but without losing our conceptual understanding. Ultimately, we will have a solid framework for analyzing the more detailed questions addressed in subsequent chapters.

In Chapter Two I will address some of the problems of macroeconomics (the top-down analysis of the economy as a whole, which includes unemployment and inflation) as opposed to microeconomics (the bottom-up analysis of households, businesses, and markets). Most non-economists are unaware that reconciling the concrete theories of microeconomics with macroeconomics has been a serious challenge for economists, one that still remains unresolved and a work-in-progress. We know how to maximize revenues and minimize costs for businesses. We're less confident when it comes to managing the entire economy with the tools of monetary policy (interest rates) and fiscal policy (taxes and government spending). (As if you needed reminding!) This is why we observe so much expert controversy over what to do with policy: should we increase the stimulus, cut taxes, or balance the budget? Raise interest rates or lower them? Take a ride on QE3? (See Quantitative Easing.)

One reason for the failures of economics, finance and related policies resides in the assumptions we make about how people behave under varying conditions of uncertainty and change. We need to improve upon the mechanical conceptualization of *homo economicus* on which economic theory is based. This conceptualization refers to the notion that businesses, or firms, always maximize profits and individuals always maximize utility (when was the last time you woke up and figured how to maximize your utility that day?);

that decision makers are well informed (we know all we need to know to make correct choices); and that individuals' and firms' preferences are fixed over time and homogeneous (or uniform) across actors (we all want basically the same thing all the time). Though these simplified notions of behavior have been very useful for building powerful and sophisticated mathematical models of markets, they fail painfully in describing many social phenomena. In this vein, I will address in some depth two keystones to developing our macroeconomic understanding: the concepts of *capital* and *risk*. How these interact with actual human behavior to shape our capitalist system will clear up a lot of common confusion.

Chapter Three addresses the fundamentals of democratic politics in the United States, from the electoral system to the organization of parties to the functioning of government. Most of us are aware that our politics are teetering on the brink of dysfunction. Unless we can make democracy work, all talk of formulating sound economic policy becomes rather superfluous. We can only briefly cover political issues, but a basic discussion is necessary in order to move on to the final two chapters. In Chapter Four we retrace some background history to the present financial and economic crisis and outline the basic principles to help orient our policy agenda.

As the preceding chapters set up the necessary tools we need to understand the dynamics of our political economy, the last, Chapter Five, becomes the meat and potatoes. We are now ready to apply our model to the most pressing policy issues going forward. These include Federal Reserve policy, entitlement reform, tax policy, and the issue of regulation, also called the principal-agent problem.

I will not address such issues as defense spending, national security, the effects of terrorism, or immigration policy. I hope this does not disappoint, but these issues depend heavily on non-economic considerations and on geopolitical issues that would require a much longer and differently focused book.

I end this guide with a recommended reading list that covers the material discussed in greater depth. For easy reference, I have also included a glossary of economic and financial terms. Many of the terms will link to Wikipedia for more focused and in-depth treatment. This book is not encyclopedic, rather it is integrative, which I believe makes it a more valuable guide.

Lastly, I welcome comments, suggestions, and/or corrections from readers. Some of the ideas presented here are controversial and open to further evaluation and interpretation. The point of participatory democracy is not necessarily to agree, but to engage. I don't presume to have all the answers, so constructive criticism or enlightened disagreement is always appreciated. These can be submitted by commenting on the discussion board at the "Casino Capitalism and Crapshoot Politics" blog or directly to the author by email:

mh@michaelharrington.info

http://casinocap.wordpress.com/

www.amazon.coom/author/michaelharrington

Author's Facebook Fan Page

Ideas are no longer cast in stone by the permanence of paper publishing and the immutable "book." As digital publishing and distribution allow frequent updates, this guide will be a living document, a work-in-progress that will periodically adapt to changes and corrections (readers can refer to version numbers). Updated e-books in your digital library can be downloaded again and again without cost from Amazon, Apple, or other distributors. I sincerely hope discussions with readers will continue to improve the presentation and clarity of the ideas discussed. Please do weigh in and help correct my errors.

CHAPTER ONE

A Simple Model

We begin our journey by constructing a rudimentary economic model that, like a vehicle, will help us navigate our analysis. Economists can't help themselves from building logical models to illustrate and order their thought processes. Whether simple or complex, these models can be extremely useful tools as they offer necessary touchstones when the analysis gets highly abstract. For our purposes we will stick to five basic building blocks for our model. Before discussing, I will list them here first. I also include the dimension of time[5] with the contextual variable of uncertainty that factors into all economic decision-making.

1. The decision of when and how much to consume, which has implications for savings and investment = **consume now or later;**
2. The opportunity to **trade (**or exchange**)** goods and services with others;
3. The role of **money** in facilitating these exchanges across time and space;
4. The option to borrow or lend through the use of **credit and debt** to shift economic decisions in time (i.e. buy now and pay later) and also to leverage the funds available for consumption, savings and investment. This introduces the concept of **interest** that governs all our inter-temporal decision-making;
5. The crucial role of **capital** and **labor** as <u>factors of production</u>;
6. Most important is the contextual variable of **uncertainty** surrounding all our decisions. This governs our perceptions of expected **risk vs. return,** i.e., what are the anticipated risks and payoffs for all possible decision options? The flip side of uncertainty is not certainty, but **confidence.**

1.1 Let's Eat! Now or Later?

All economics really flows from one key concept: *the simple decision of whether to consume today or tomorrow* (whereby tomorrow indicates some indefinite point in the future). When you think about it, economics is founded on biology and human psychological behavior. Life is generated by the act of consuming, as all organisms go through the lifecycle of feeding, growing, reproducing, and dying. So, the desire, or imperative, to consume is fundamental to all economic analysis. We can observe our acquisitive nature very early in child development with some of the first words of a two-year-old: "mine," "I want," "give me," and "more." This is basic biology. It's no wonder we humans are such good consumers—it's in our DNA.

You might ask: Don't we have to produce something before we can consume it? But this just recalls the chicken or the egg paradox of which comes first.[6] Our ancestors on this planet were consumers long before they were producers. Hunter and gatherer societies lived from hand to mouth until they learned how to preserve meat and cultivate grains. Such "technologies" allowed these societies to overproduce relative to immediate consumption needs and to save the surplus for the proverbial "rainy day." You may also have the perception that you produce primarily to provide for your family and leave a legacy for your progeny, but this just means that at some point in the future somebody else will be consuming what you produce today. The purpose of all production is eventual consumption (because, really, you can't take it with you and there's no reason to produce unless the product is eventually going to be consumed).[7]

What we don't consume now is saved, but it can also be "invested" in production, thus increasing our stock of goods for later consumption. This simple decision problem of what to consume now, and what to save and invest in order to consume later, is where human psychology enters the economic equation.

Let us consider the simple decisions facing a farmer at harvest time: how much corn to consume and how much seed corn to put aside (save) for next season, to eat then or plant (invest) for another harvest. If the farmer's family consumes all the corn during the first winter, they will grow fat and happy but could face starvation when the grain runs out. If they save all the corn for next year's planting, they will surely starve before they can even get it in the ground. This process implies a kind of balance of flows across time: this year's harvest flows into next year's, which flows into the following year, and so on. Like the farmer, we too seek to find an *equilibrium* level that allocates our resources between present *consumption* and *saving* to yield the 'crop' we need to harvest next year, all the while making sure we have a comfortable cushion of 'stored corn' to consume through the winter. The more we save and invest 'seed corn,' the larger our total harvest grows (to a point). Anything that upsets this delicate balance will threaten our long-term survival and that of our families and communities.[8] This logic applies equally to the entire world economy. Today's consumption demands support today's production levels (i.e., the people who eat corn keep the farmer in production); today's savings supports today's investment in future production (the farmer's seed corn is saved and reinvested in next year's crop); and that future production provides for an increased level of future consumption (another bountiful crop feeds more people next season). This is how market societies grow their economies. It can be a virtuous cycle, or a vicious one when reversed. Think of how growing inequality and rising unemployment can reverse this cycle by undermining present consumption, making new investment in production superfluous.

1.2 I Like What You Have - Let's Trade

Our proverbial farmer does not need to survive on corn alone if he is a member of a wider community. He can take some of his corn and trade it for wheat, vegetables, honey, or whatever else other farmers or tradesmen produce. This establishes the concept of an exchange rate, or price, for corn relative to other goods and services. Trade is an important concept in economics. It allows us to specialize in what we do best and then offer the goods or services we produce in return for ones that others specialize in producing. This process of specialization increases our productive efficiency and makes everybody better off. This is true for farmers within a community, or for nations in the world market.[9] The desire to trade led to the development of markets. These markets introduced us to the economic concepts of supply and demand, where supply represents what we produce and sell, while demand represents what we buy and consume. The quantities supplied and demanded will balance at the correct market price of the good, often called the *equilibrium price*.

We will discuss in greater depth how markets work, but the general idea should be fairly obvious to anyone who shops in a supermarket. No longer do we have to grow our own produce or raise and slaughter our own livestock in order to put food on the table. And somehow, after buying all the food we can eat, we still have money left over to go to the movies, perhaps in a new car.

1.3 I Need Some $Money$

The development of trade led to the evolution of money. It is difficult to barter in cows, chickens, and bushels of wheat, so early trading civilizations developed substitute goods that could represent comparable values. Some were as simple as shells or cigarettes, but soon evolved into precious coins and letters of credit. Money as we know it, whether coins, bills, or checks drawn on banks, has becomes the universal measure of relative value. We price things in money and exchange money for goods and services.

The functional definition of money has three components: it is a *medium of exchange*, a *unit of account*, and a *store of value*. First, coins and bills are easier to take to market for exchange than the physical goods we want to trade. Second, we price things in a single unit of account—in the U.S. it is dollars and cents—and use this to compare values. And, third, our money (when deposited in a cookie jar, a bank, or invested) becomes a way to preserve purchasing power for the future.

We will discuss money in great depth throughout this guide, but the most important question concerns how we determine the currency's value. For instance, what determines the value of a U.S. dollar bill? The answer may seem obvious, but it isn't.[10] Our natural fascination with money sometimes obscures the fact that government-issued currency (called fiat currency) is only worth what it will buy. It was different when we used goats, cows, camels, or gold as currency because these other currencies (called commodity money or specie) also had utilitarian value. You can always milk or eat a cow or wear gold jewelry. A dollar, however, is only as valuable as whatever else it can be exchanged for. This is a bit more complex than it sounds, and is very easy to misunderstand. Consider the fact that we can't really buy anything in France with a US$, except euros. We have to exchange dollars for euros before we can buy any croissants, cheese, or wine. Similarly, we cannot buy Italian wine with dollars, only with euros. If you buy an Italian wine in a U.S. shop, the importer, or exporter, has already exchanged dollars for euros. Another way of putting this is that as wine flows from Tuscany to New York, dollars are sold and euros bought. Same thing with Mercedes cars and French cheeses. A dollar can only be directly exchanged for goods denominated in dollars, i.e., U.S. assets or goods made in the good ole U.S.A. The value of a dollar is thus determined by all the goods and services available to buy with dollars, divided by the total stock of dollars.[11]

Supposedly, the supply of a currency is controlled by a country's central bank. In the U.S., it's called the Federal Reserve.[12] Because a country's money consists of far more than bills in circulation, the actual supply and who controls it is a matter of serious debate. In the next chapter, in the section titled, The Mystique of Money, we will discover that whoever controls the supply of money holds the ultimate power to determine its value. You may be surprised at what we find.

1.4 Debt and Credit

The utility of money introduces the instruments of debt and credit and the concepts of borrowing and lending into our model. First, let us not get confused by the terms debt and credit, as they both refer to the same thing from opposing perspectives. Credit originates, or is issued, by a lender or a bond buyer; debt is incurred by the borrower or bond issuer. For example, when a business extends you credit, you assume it as debt.

Borrowing and lending are most often conducted through financial intermediaries (i.e., banks) and help redistribute consumption across space and time. For instance, I can borrow on credit to increase my present consumption, but the debt incurred also requires less consumption in the future in order to pay back the loan. I can also borrow on credit to invest in production that will increase my income in the future so that I can pay back the loan without shrinking future consumption. The key is *whether the investment in the present increases income in the future.* If it does and we can pay back the debt with interest, then we are richer for the debt assumed. But if our product and our incomes do not increase, the credit has only enabled us to borrow consumption and savings from the future, which will be bleaker for it. For example, if instead of getting more education, I borrow to buy a fancy sports car that doesn't help me increase my income, then I will be poorer for it in the future because I will have to pay back the loan (with interest). Most people understand this intuitively and as it relates to them personally, but it also applies on the national scale, though there are crucial differences between individuals and governments.[13]

On the opposite side of borrowers are savers and lenders. Savers and lenders defer present consumption in order to receive returns on their loans to borrowers, which will increase the savers' and lenders' incomes in the future. This borrowing and lending relationship applies not only to bank loans but also to the issuance of bonds or mortgages. Bonds and mortgages are nothing more than debt instruments that specify an agreement to borrow a certain amount of money to be paid back over a certain time period with interest. Borrowing and lending, and saving and investing represent an exchange of 'goods' just like any other market transaction. The price of this 'good' is established by the various rates of interest specified in the terms. The bank, or financial intermediary, is nothing more than the middleman between buyer and seller. The balance, or equilibrium, between the supply and demand for funds is maintained over time by the *interest rate.*[14]

There is no need to complicate our model unnecessarily at this point, but it is important to understand the complete role interest rates play in our simple model. The interest rate not only affects the level of savings and investment, but also the levels of production and consumption over time. Interest rates, whether 2% or 5% or 15%, influence our decisions because they change the relative values of present vs. future consumption. A high interest rate encourages us to save, thus deferring consumption and reducing borrowing. Conversely, a low interest rate encourages us to consume now and borrow, since the pay-off received for deferring consumption is low. Because we value present consumption over future consumption (this is rational, not only do we value instant gratification, but life is unpredictable), the interest rate that tips the balance in our decision between present or future consumption is often called the *time value* of money. (The interest rate will also reflect the risk premium to the lender in case the borrower cannot repay, and the inflation premium[15] if the lender anticipates future price inflation, which would reduce the value of the money he was repaid.)

The interest received by individual savers for lending money is the interest paid by borrowers for the use of their savings. If rates are high, there are fewer borrowers and more savers, and the rate must fall if savers want to attract more borrowers. If they are low, there are more borrowers and fewer savers, and the rate must rise. For borrowers and investors, the level of interest rates influences the cost of capital and how profitable their investments have to be to justify the risk of borrowing and lending. If it costs me 10% interest to borrow funds, my investment has to return more than 10% or I will lose money. Consumption that is deferred into savings that are then profitably invested in new production leads to an increase in the stock of wealth. We call this increase *economic growth*.

Economists have documented some natural patterns in the ebbs and flows of consumption, savings, investment, and production. One is the "lifecycle hypothesis" that shows greater consumption and lower savings at the beginning and at the end of life, among the young and the old. Saving and producing is maximized during the middle phase of our lives. So, the consumption pattern of the entire population will be influenced by the demographic distribution of that population. In the U.S., this has been most noticeable with the economic boom associated with the postwar baby boom generation in its most productive middle-aged years. As baby-boomers enter their retirement years, their consumption levels will increase.

Another natural pattern is associated with the evolution of technology. Consider, for example, the impacts of the industrial revolution, the development of such technologies as the railroads, steel production, electricity, the automobile, telegraph and telephone, airplane transportation and, more recently, the development of the microchip, the personal computer, and the Internet. During periods of technological advancement, consumption is deferred as investment is poured into new productive opportunities. This is facilitated by rising interest rates, increased saving, increased productivity and economic growth. Technology also changes the mix of capital and labor in the production process as it increases labor productivity. Think of how the personal computer has eliminated the need for the office typing pool.

These two cyclical patterns of demographics—or population growth—and technological progress are the true determinants of economic growth. A rising population supplies more workers to produce, while technological innovation causes more investment, combining capital with labor and increasing the productivity of both. The result is greater national wealth. It would appear that the political goal of economic policy should be to promote a larger working population and foster technological innovation. If it were only that simple.

Not surprisingly, government policies seek to accelerate these two natural cyclical patterns with the goal of stimulating economic growth. The road to wealth, however, is not guaranteed only by a higher birth rate or larger population. Otherwise, China and India would be the world's richest nations. Demographic trends respond to much larger sociological and economic factors and cannot be easily manipulated in the short-term through government policy.[16] The more important policy goal is to put the population to productive work, and this is where technological progress comes in. Technological innovation thrives in an environment of freedom and confidence-inspired risk-taking. The government can do much to insure these conditions through attention to property rights, the rule of law, civil rights, a judicial system, and functioning capital markets. These are the institutional structures that serve to ensure the sustainability of economic growth through time.

However, because politics demands more immediate results, we are often given short-term fixes that yield very mixed outcomes. Many of us are aware that the Federal Reserve Bank manipulates interest rates in order to promote certain policy objectives, such as full employment and increased economic growth. This manipulation is not always an unqualified great idea. For instance, if the interest rate is subsidized too low, people can consume more by borrowing cheaply, rather than dipping into their own savings. In other words, they can max out the credit card. Artificially low interest rates result in increased savings, investment, and consumption all at the same time! Our basic economic decision is no longer consumption now *OR* later, but consumption now *AND* later. If this sounds too good to be true, that's because it is. Unproductive ideas get funded along with productive ones while the bill for increased borrowing always comes due. This should sound familiar. It is the root cause of the enormous credit bubble that has been building for the past three decades, leading to the financial meltdown in 2008.

1.5 Capital vs. Labor: Friends or Foes?

Capital and labor are defined as <u>factors of production</u>. We labor, or work, in order to produce something and we use capital to leverage our labor. Capital is any resource that is put to productive use (this will be explained more thoroughly in the section on <u>Capital and Financial Markets</u> in Chapter Two). The farmer may work with a hoe all day long but can still only till a small field. But with a tractor, or fleet of tractors and farmhands, he may be able to cultivate many acres of crops. The physical capital of the tractors is financed by financial capital, while the expertise of farming becomes a store of human capital. We combine these factors as inputs into the production process. Then we pay out the costs of employing the various inputs with shares received from the sale of the output.

To demonstrate, let us consider the simple business of baking and selling a pie. First we need capital, either our own savings or perhaps a loan from the bank, to pay for the ingredients and other costs upfront. We need milk, flour, butter, sugar, fruit, chocolate or vanilla flavoring, etc. and we pay for these ingredients according to the prices they command in the marketplace. Then we either use our own labor or pay a pastry chef. We also need an oven, preferably in a kitchen with a supply of water. After we bake the pie we can sell the pieces and use the proceeds to pay back the bank or investor who financed the cash payments to buy the inputs. Hopefully, at the end of the day there is some pie left over, which we can either eat ourselves or sell for a profit.

Notice here that the sale of the pie is ultimately what will cover the payments for the chef and the ingredients, which were paid out before the pie was ever sold. If the pie had been spoiled, the loss would have been borne by the baking entrepreneur, who would still have to pay back the bank or default on the loan. Thus, there is financial risk here borne by both the bank and the entrepreneur. This introduces the important concept of risk and return: Investment *risk* is an additional factor of production that must be compensated with an expected positive return. The banker receives an interest premium on the loan to compensate him for the risk of default, and the successful baking entrepreneur earns a residual profit to reward her for the overall risk of the business venture. The greater the potential risk of loss, the greater the expected return for success. Note that certain inputs took little or no risk – the sellers of the flour or butter or sugar or even the chef – thus, their share of the product is minimal. They make their money on volume as all pies made require a certain amount of inputs that add up to a significant market for the sale of these inputs.

There are two important elements of this process to note. First, that the prices of inputs are set by the supply and demand for these inputs. If there were only one cup of sugar but many pounds of flour available to five bakers who all wanted to make and sell pies, then the price of sugar would be much higher relative to the price of flour. The same applies to the supply and demand for chefs, or labor, as well as the supply and demand for capital. If required labor is scarce, it can command a higher share of output through a higher wage. If capital is scarce, it can command a higher share of profits relative to the payouts to other factors of production. The risk of loss assumed by the capital investor will also factor into the cost of capital. Thus, the higher the credit risk of the baker, the higher the interest rate the bank will charge on the loan.

The second important point concerns the flip side of input prices— indicating how the final product of the wealth-creating process is distributed. We can calculate how much of the total income created by the baking enterprise is received by the sellers of ingredients, the chef, the bank, and the baking entrepreneur. When firms are highly profitable and growing, the entrepreneur/owner will receive a larger share of the pie. These profits can grow or shrink depending on outside competition from additional bakers. Of course, if the business fails the hired chef has received her last paycheck and the business will be buying no more ingredients. The initial payments to these costs become part of the loss incurred by the baking entrepreneur, and possibly the bank.

This simple analogy illustrates how the capitalist production process determines the relationship between capital and labor. The chef cannot command a higher wage unless there is a shortage of chefs or a new technology is introduced that increases her productivity. Otherwise, the chef's raise will result in higher prices for pies, less labor employed, or will force the baker into closing the business because of inadequate profits. The crucial difference between the chef and the entrepreneurial bakery owner is *who assumes the burden of risk* for the success or failure of the enterprise. Whoever assumes the bulk of the risk, will receive the requisite compensating share of the reward.

Another way to look at this is to think of the production process as an equation. On one side we have the value of the final product less all the costs of production. On the other side we have the residual profits. So, revenues minus costs equal profits:

$$REVENUES - COSTS = PROFITS$$

Any kid with a lemonade stand can figure this out. We take the money received from the sale of the lemonade and subtract the cost of the lemons and the labor and we are left with profit or loss. In this equation, prepaid labor is on the cost side of the equation and owner-entrepreneurs are on the profit side. Businesses succeed by raising profits and lowering costs, so the success of the capitalist economy is enhanced by lower labor costs yielding higher profits to risk-taking investment.

This might suggest that labor is in a weak or losing bargaining position relative to capital, i.e. the more labor loses, the more capital gains (Marxist conflict is rooted in this idea). But this is not necessarily true over time. As profits rise, more entrepreneurs enter the business to capture those profits. They will employ additional labor, increasing demand relative to supply and driving up the price (wages/salaries) of labor.

More importantly, what our baking example does show is that *risk* of loss is a factor of capitalist production that must be paid for. Whoever successfully assumes the risk will gain a share of the reward. This should give us a clue as to the role of Wall Street and its securities markets in our economy. Capital markets help us manage risk in more efficient ways by distributing it far and wide. If a venture is successful, this assumption of risk commands a positive return. This is how a high-flying hedge fund manager can make almost $4 billion in one year – by making large risky gambles with borrowed capital that ultimately pay off. There is nothing depraved or scandalous about this. (Of course, none of these gambles should ever be bailed out by taxpayers when they fail – the game of "heads we win, tails you lose" *is* arguably an unfair and immoral one.)

1.6 Risk, Return and Uncertainty

In Section 1 above we briefly discussed consumption and acquisitiveness as the fundamental building block, or behavioral assumption, of economic analysis. Some have disparaged this human impulse as greed and avarice, and certainly it can be described so in the extreme. But the impulse is instinctual for a very good reason. We need resources to survive, so, by nature, it is imperative to acquire these resources by hook or by crook. This is no more of a moral choice than that of a lion eating a gazelle. More important is the logic that drives our desire to acquire is the even stronger in our fear of losing what we have. We refer to this possibility as *risk*.

The concept of risk is fundamental to understanding how our political economy and society work. In a world of constant change, risk is ubiquitous. (The alternative—a world that never changed—would mean we were frozen in time with no risk *and* no reward.) Because change is unpredictable, or uncertain, we are never sure how it might affect us or whether it will threaten our well-being. There is the dual possibility that change will be either good for us or will be bad for us. As a consequence, our natural survival instincts have made us very sensitive to the threat of uncertainty and loss. For this reason, many people innately fear change, and their fears are not merely the flip side of acquisitiveness, they are far more acute. With experimental studies, behavioral scientists have shown that test subjects are twice as sensitive to a possible loss than they are to a possible gain. We call this behavior *loss aversion*. (See note.[17])

Loss aversion is a critical concept that governs our psychological behavior. Imagine two patrons enter a Las Vegas casino. The first gambler has $10 to bet and the second has $100, so the second is 10 times richer than the first. They both wager at the blackjack table and the first wins $10 while the second loses $80. Now they both have $20, but imagine how they feel. The first patron, having doubled his money, leaves feeling flush and hails a cab in a moment of extravagance. The second, normally a free spender, feels impoverished and hoards his $20, choosing to walk. These two gamblers now have the same endowment and economic theory would expect them to behave the same. But their histories and their psychological experiences differ and so, accordingly, does their economic behavior. This has been amply demonstrated through behavioral studies.[18]

The concept of uncertainty is related to risk, but is not the same thing. Uncertainty is the unpredictability, or variability, of any particular outcome;

risk is the probability of actual material loss. The movement of stock prices is very uncertain from day to day, but if we don't own shares these gyrations present little risk of loss to us (unless our employer goes bankrupt).

The state of the world is uncertain and our most primal behavioral responses are reactions to uncertainty and the risk of potential loss. This is why I argue that risk and uncertainty are the keys to understanding economic choices and outcomes and that risk is the glue that holds our economic models together.

No matter how much we seek to avoid losses, we cannot avoid the ever-present risks we face due to events outside our control. Often the best we can do is to shift various risks around, seeking to manage them in ways that enhance our survival. Our ancestors moved into caves to protect themselves from the elements and wild beasts. They built walled cities and defensive weaponry to protect themselves from invaders. In modern times we take self-defense classes, adopt workplace and environmental standards, and establish Social Security and Medicare for the same reasons. All through our lives we seek to manage risks and avoid losses, hoping to live to enjoy another day. But even if we could, we would never completely eliminate economic risks because *without risk there is no reward* in life. We are motivated to seek gains subject to an acceptable level of risk and if risks and returns are too low, we will seek out bigger risk-taking gambles to manage in search of larger gains.

Managing risks, not avoiding them, is how we gain the rewards that life offers. Because risk is a *negative good* (in economic parlance, a *good* is something we will pay to obtain), we will pay someone to take it off our hands. This is why we pay premiums to insurance companies to compensate us if we suffer a loss. We pay them to absorb the risk of loss. If the loss never occurs the insurer pockets the premium and reinvests it. The insurer can assume these risks because it diversifies the risks it is assuming across a large risk pool of clients. Turning this logic on its head, when we assume risks ourselves and are successful in managing them, we can receive the payoff.

There is actually a direct relationship between risk and return: the higher the risk, the higher the expected return; and vice versa, the lower the risk, the lower the return. This relationship between risk and return is called the "return-to-risk ratio" or the "risk-adjusted rate of return" (RAR). In theory, the RAR is the same for all investments and in practice all RARs will revert to that mean. This is just another way of saying that if an investment's RAR is higher than an alternative investment, investors will prefer the higher and bid up the price of the investment until the higher RAR reverts to the average RAR.[19] Think about this: If you pay more for an investment while the expected return stays the same, the RAR ratio must fall.

The most obvious illustration of the equivalence of RARs is a roulette table, where all the odds of different gambling strategies are virtually equivalent. If they were not, smart gamblers would only play the best odds ratios. Imagine if black paid off at 3 to 1 and red paid off at 2 to 1, yet there are equal numbers of red and black outcomes on the roulette wheel, so your chance of red vs. black is 50-50, but the payoff for black is 50% higher. Who, except the most mathematically challenged and blind, would play red until the RAR was adjusted so the payoffs were the same? Understanding risk and return can help explain many economic phenomena.

I stated above that uncertainty is the natural state of an unpredictable universe, but there is a variability of uncertainty in our lives. An approaching storm greatly increases the level of uncertainty governing our sense of well-being compared to a clear blue sky. The uncertainty of war is another example of uncontrolled uncertainty and risk. A commonplace economic uncertainty arises from price inflation and currency depreciation. Long term investment is greatly complicated if one does not have confidence in the value of the currency in the future. This is reflected in the nervous trading in gold over the past few years. Another case of uncertainty gathers around politics. What kind of impact will different political outcomes have on our economic well-being? Uncertainties associated with specific policy platforms will affect our longer-term economic decisions.

The flipside of uncertainty is confidence. When uncertainty over the future decreases, the level of confidence increases for successfully managing risks and profiting from change. The perception of these two subjective variables of uncertainty and confidence has a profound affect on the material value of capital. The more confident we are in the future, the greater we value capital; the more uncertain or fearful we are, the less we value capital. This is why, in the midst of a crisis, political leaders are wont to assure us that "the only thing we have to fear is fear itself." In capital markets, we'll see that fear can be self-fulfilling.

By introducing some basic concepts, we have developed a simple model of the political economy that we can apply to various political and economic questions. As we will be using these concepts extensively, let us summarize:

All economic decisions are rooted in the decision of whether to **consume now or later**. Present consumption deferred is essentially saving, and our savings become a store of future value against risk (i.e. saving for a rainy day) or can be made available for investment. The decisions to consume or save, to invest or produce, are influenced by many factors, but primarily by the **interest rate**. A high interest rate discourages consumption, promotes saving, and indicates a strong demand for investment funds. A low interest rate encourages consumption, discourages saving, and indicates a weak demand for investment. Varying levels of investment and production reflect the possibilities of earning a return higher than the cost of borrowing. An expected positive return will increase investment and production. An expected negative return will have the opposite effect.

Individual economic decisions about consuming are linked together by opportunities to **trade goods and services**. This trade is facilitated by **money** in the form of a common currency that is easily exchanged for goods and services and convertible into other currencies.

Credit and **debt,** utilizing financial intermediaries like banks and securities exchanges, allow us to distribute our economic decisions across time and space. When presented with a promising investment opportunity, we don't need to wait until we save enough capital. Rather we can borrow it from other savers through the capital markets and pay it back in the future.

Capital and **labor** are the two primary factors of production that, when productively employed allow us to increase our levels of consumption and wealth over time. The cost of capital and the price of labor also determine how the product of wealth creation is shared across society. If the price of labor is high and the cost of capital is low, labor will receive a greater share of production and vice-versa.

Another important factor in the production process is the **return to risk (or RAR),** usually reflected in the cost of capital. Risk also determines how product is distributed between factors of production as higher risk-taking commands higher expected returns if successful.

All economic and financial decisions are heavily influenced by the subjective nature of **uncertainty** over the future and our **confidence** in predicting that future.

Naturally, there are many additional factors that influence our basic economic decisions and shape our society. The more we introduce, the more complex our analytical challenge becomes. The few offered here, however, are sufficient for analyzing and understanding many of the economic issues salient to our lives. I have included a more technical, but succinct, summary of this consumption model in Appendix A.

CHAPTER TWO

The Macroeconomy

Most non-economists would probably be alarmed to learn that there is so much disagreement among economists with regard to macroeconomic theory and practice. This state of affairs contrasts sharply with that of microeconomic theory, which is concerned with how firms maximize profits and consumers maximize utility. Business owners are fairly clear on how to best increase their revenues, reduce costs, minimize the cost of capital, and manage risks in order to maximize their profits. Average consumers are also aware of how to manage their personal budgets, shop for the best prices, and allocate spending and saving behavior so they do not end up destitute (well, maybe not all consumers). In extrapolating microeconomic analysis to the macroeconomy, it is far less apparent that economic experts know what is happening until after the fact, or even if they comprehend it correctly at all. The recent financial and economic crisis, with its resultant policy controversies, only reinforces such doubts.

Assumptions about how rational individuals behave when faced with the straightforward task of increasing their incomes do not always lend themselves so easily to understanding how populations of millions of people attempt to navigate an unpredictable world. Businesspeople can confidently anticipate their local markets, products, and customers, yet fumble in the dark when it comes to anticipating where the entire economy is headed, especially when the macroeconomy is influenced by so many factors outside their control. Wars break out, natural disasters occur, public policies change on a political whim. All these factors have profound effects on the aggregate economic decisions of the entire population. Macroeconomic uncertainty and risk play a significant role in the decision-making of all market participants.

In order to have a basic understanding how the economy works, it may be helpful to think of the macroeconomy as a living organism made up of billions of individual cells. Through each of its billions of cells, this organism consumes, saves, invests, and produces. What it produces today is what it will consume, save, and invest tomorrow and so on into the future. So the economy must constantly recycle its product in order to grow. It (all of us together) recycles its product by constantly consuming, saving, investing, and producing in balanced proportions in order to sustain itself over time. If it fails, it will become unstable and be forced to correct itself or be corrected.[20]

People seem to grasp this concept most easily when it is applied to environmental concerns. If we deplete (i.e. consume) the planet's natural resources and create nothing more, our civilization will soon perish. Let's see how sustainability applies to our simple economic exchange model. The watchwords for a sustainable market exchange economy are 1) balance, 2) coordination, and 3) pace. Perhaps the best analogy is to a marathon runner. Both legs must operate in tandem and coordinate in time in order to run the fastest while still staying upright. Then the runner must set a pace that is sustainable for twenty-six miles. If one leg gets too far out in front of the other, both get out of sync and the result is a face plant. If the pace is too fast, the runner will collapse exhausted. The two legs of the economy are supply and demand. It's heart and lungs are the financial industry. The financial crisis of 2008 was our collapse and face plant.

Remember the case of the farmer. If he consumes too much now without saving enough to replant next year, his current harvest will be his last and his family will be driven off the farm, perhaps eventually to starve. In the same way, if everyone consumes too much now, there will be insufficient saving and investment for tomorrow's consumption needs. Excess production to meet today's consumer demand will in time decline for lack of reinvestment, and the economy will slow. On the other hand, if we defer consumption too much in order to save, there will be excess funds available for investment, but insufficient demand today to justify putting those investment funds into new production. Investment returns will plunge, asset prices will rise as they are bid up by the excess investment funds, and the economy will shrink. As the economy shrinks, so will future demand, causing those asset prices that rose to fall again reflecting the economy's losses and devaluation of capital.

We need just the right flows of consumption, savings, and productive investment over time in order to keep the economic system on a steady, sustainable path. But how can we determine the proper proportions for consuming now and later? This seems an impossible task to get right. It is possible, however, as sure as the world turns, if all economic decisions are guided by a functioning price system, with the most important price being the *interest rate*.

Economists have come to recognize that one of the most important functions of markets is the information value of their price signals that give *feedback* to producers, consumers, savers, and investors about what choices to make and which actions to take. The centralized command economies of the 20th century—those of the USSR or China, for instance—had no chance to perform this function, as their bureaucrats gave input and output directives to producers. One popular anecdote concerns the Soviet central planner who issued a directive for a ton of nails that would be needed for building. Naturally, the size of a nail matters for construction, but the factory fulfilled the order with twenty *one hundred pound* nails! What does one do with a hundred pound nail? That was not the central planner's problem. The market feedback from those companies that needed the nails for construction were not taken into account.

Another amusing anecdote describes a Western economist's experience surveying the construction of a large dam in China. He was surprised to see thousands of workers using shovels. Suggesting that the work would progress much faster with tractors and large earth movers, he was told that doing the work with shovels helped to increase employment. "I see," said the economist, "I thought you were trying to build a dam. If you want to maximize employment, you should use teaspoons!"

Open and competitive markets provide the most accurate price signals to market participants to insure that they make the right decisions. This fact is fairly uncontroversial and is widely accepted by all economists. The tougher question is: Why do markets fail?

2.1 Market Failures

There is a wealth of sophisticated economics studies into market failures, but we might better understand the basic issues with recourse to some simple logic and intuition. How does a functioning and self-correcting market work? The market feedback process follows the famous law of supply and demand, where supply and demand are brought into balance at what is called the equilibrium price. If the price deviates from this equilibrium, actions by buyers and sellers work to bring it back to the correct price to clear the market where supply equals demand. We experience this market rationalization every day. As consumers, we desire a particular good and are willing and able to pay a certain price for it. Producers are guided by the cost of manufacturing the good, their risks, and expected profits. If the price consumers are willing to pay is sufficient to cover the cost plus deliver a return on the risk-taking investment, producers can be assured a <u>profit</u>. Given an anticipated price, the producer offers a certain supply for sale. If the product inventory sells out, he can raise his price on the next batch or just increase production, whichever maximizes his total profits.

On the other hand, if buyers decide that the price the producer sets is too high, the producer will have left-over inventory. This negative feedback tells him he must lower his price and/or reduce production. As buyers and sellers meet in the marketplace and make trades everyday, their preferences are soon reflected in the prices and the quantities of goods exchanged. Market equilibrium is insured by a negative feedback process, whereby market participants respond to price deviations with actions that bring the price back to equilibrium. Anybody who shops for "sales" is enacting this negative feedback process. We know how well these market processes work when we walk into the supermarket and decide what to buy from its incredible array of choices. If you ever meet someone who has grown up in an un-free or non-market society, you will find that the first thing they marvel over is a modern supermarket stocked with foods from all over the world. They have never experienced anything like this because a society without market feedback has stores with empty shelves, long lines, and ration cards for the scant goods that do become available.

We should note here that labor also operates as a feedback exchange market with the wage being the equilibrium price that balances the supply and demand for labor at different skill levels.

Normally, goods and services markets rarely fail. Sometimes there are supply shocks, such as the 1970s oil embargo, during which the supply of oil was cut off and its price skyrocketed. Similarly, severe weather or droughts that affect the grain harvest will lead to spikes in the price of food. But these are not market failures, they are market shocks. Markets respond with negative feedback and the market soon returns to equilibrium.

One example of a true market failure is a <u>natural monopoly</u>, which results from efficiencies gained through large-scale production. The larger a company gets, the easier to beat the competition, leading to monopolistic pricing power.[21] Think of an electric power company or the original Bell telephone company.

Another important market failure is when costs are not included in the price of the good. Consider the pollution produced as a by-product of industrial manufacturing. The cost of the pollution is not paid by the producer or consumer but is borne by those who suffer from the pollution and its secondary effects. For example, increased lung disease by coal miners may be the cost they pay for cheaper energy prices for consumers and higher profits for coal mining companies. We call these types of failures <u>externalities</u>.

A third market failure concerns <u>public goods</u>, such as the military. In economics, public goods have very specific conditions that differentiate them from private goods. It is important to understand this distinction. Private and public goods are *not* defined as goods provided either by private companies or by the government. Public goods, in fact, are defined as non-rival in consumption and non-excludable. Non-rival means that my consumption of the good does not affect yours, and yours does not affect mine. Non-excludable means that I cannot exclude you from consuming the good, thus I have no power to actually make you pay for it. A good example of a public good is clean air, the more I breath does not reduce the amount you can breath and I cannot exclude you from breathing the same air. On the other hand, a juicy steak is not a public good. If I eat it, you cannot. If I produce the beef, I can exclude you from partaking in its consumption. Private goods can be produced, priced and paid for; public goods cannot. The private market will not provide public goods because they cannot price such goods, receive payment, or prevent people from free-riding. The private market fails because the desired good is not produced and consumed.

We can easily see how this applies to national defense. If someone else pays for the U.S. Navy to protect the nation (through taxes?), as a U.S. resident I still get the same protection, even if I don't pay taxes. So, the federal government provides for our mutual protection as a public good paid for out of general tax revenues they do collect. A private navy could not provide this good unless they had the power to tax. (Unfortunately, we have convinced ourselves that old-age pensions and healthcare are public goods, even though they have been provided for by private markets for centuries.)

In general, most market failures can be traced to some form of *information failure* whereby faulty price signals do not bring the market into equilibrium through the feedback process. A good example is the used car market, where the seller knows the true value of the automobile and the buyer does not. If the car is a lemon, the seller has an incentive to hide this fact and pass the car off to an unsuspecting borrower at a high price. Buyers are aware of this possibility and offer a lower price. If the car is truly a good value, the seller refuses to lower the price. Only if it is a lemon does he lower it in order to make a fair sale. So people keep good cars, refusing to sell them cheaply, and lemons tend to dominate sales in the used car market, which is why so many people are willing to pay more for dealer guarantees.

By and large, goods markets that are open to competition will adjust quickly to changing conditions and maintain equilibrium between supply and demand. The consumer goods we buy every day rarely fluctuate wildly in price day to day or disappear permanently from the store shelves. In the capitalist macroeconomy the most crucial markets are those for labor and capital, both of which are vulnerable to frequent market failures. But before we tackle capital and labor markets, we must address the mysteries of money.

2.2 The Mystique of Money

In the previous chapter we briefly introduced the concept of money as one of the essential building blocks of our simple model. We also stated that the most important but confusing question about money concerns its value. Unfortunately, the mystique of money is perpetuated by a monetary system that is shrouded in secrecy and obscured by complexity.

We'll begin with a simple U.S. $1 bill. What is it good for? Well, it can be exchanged for real goods, say, anything in the 99 cent store. It can also be deposited into a bank savings account to receive interest over time. Its value will derive from these functions as a medium of exchange and a store of value. (Aside from these functions, a piece of green paper, as opposed to a gold coin, has no intrinsic, or real, value. Some may argue a hunk of shiny metal has no intrinsic value either, but that argument is unconvincing to at least the female half of the population.) A fiat currency's true value is determined by what it can be exchanged for, either now or later. The theoretical value of one U.S. dollar is the total of all dollar assets divided by the total supply of dollars. So value = sum of assets divided by sum of currency supply. Let's unravel these concepts.

We consider dollar value as an asset when it's in our wallet or savings account. This is because a dollar represents a claim on real assets—we can buy something with it. An interesting question is: since a dollar is a claim, who bears the liability for this claim?

Prior to 1933, one could take a U.S. dollar bill and redeem gold from the U.S. Treasury. The liability of the dollar bill was then borne by the U.S. government, backed by its gold supply. The saying that once described the US$ was, "Good as gold." In 1933, the U.S. government, by <u>executive order</u> of President Roosevelt, outlawed the private ownership of gold coin and bullion, demanding that gold held by U.S. citizens be redeemed for dollars at the rate of $35 per ounce. Foreign governments, not subject to U.S. laws, could continue to hold and redeem dollars for gold from the U.S. Treasury at the rate of $35 per ounce. By 1971, foreign gold redemptions threatened to clean out the U.S. gold supply (we'll discuss how later), forcing President Nixon to close the Treasury's "gold window." From that point on, the U.S. government has repudiated any redemption liability for U.S. paper currency, merely designating the dollar as legal tender for payment of goods and services, backed by "the full faith and credit" of the U.S. government. In 1974, President Ford lifted the private ban on gold coins and bullion. This history demonstrates how the U.S. dollar monetary system was transformed from a commodity exchange standard (dollars to gold) to a pure fiat standard.

So, where did the liability go?

Actually, the liability stayed right where it was, it was just transformed. The gold reserves held by the U.S. Treasury were always technically the property of the U.S. citizenry. It was *our* gold stored there in Fort Knox, supposedly held in trust and guarded by our political institutions. Under a fiat currency, the liability for the U.S. dollar is still borne by the citizenry through the value of their assets and their productivity. Every citizen of the U.S. backs up the *full faith and credit* of the U.S. dollar with our ability to pay off all dollar debts incurred, either now or in the future. A foreigner holding a U.S. dollar has a claim to exchange it for U.S. goods and services—he can buy a house, a business, or even Rockefeller Center. (As of 2011, the Chinese government holds roughly $1.1 trillion of claims on the U.S. Treasury.)

We may think the supply of dollars is represented by the quantity of dollar bills and coins floating around the economy—in our wallets, cash registers, and piggy banks. But this is not really true. The bills in our wallets are just for the convenience of small purchases. We pay for most purchases not with physical paper money, but with checks drawn on bank demand deposits (a fancy word for a checking account). Paper bills and coins only represent a small fraction of our actual money, the bulk is in the form of electronic credits on bank statements. For those unfamiliar with banking, perhaps the next disclosure will be the eye-opener: the *commercial banking system,* regulated by the Federal Reserve, creates the money supply by issuing new credits in the form of loans. Let's see how this works.

When you deposit $1000 in your bank checking or savings account, your bank is permitted to take that money and lend it out again to borrowers. The bank is only required by Federal Reserve regulations to keep 10% as a capital reserve in case depositors should want their money. Since most people leave their money safely in the bank, 10% is considered an adequate reserve on hand under normal circumstances. Keeping $100 in reserve, the bank makes a $900 loan. But as that loan money is spent, where does it go? Right back to the bank in somebody else's account. The bank can the lend out 90% of that new deposit, or $810. If we keep reiterating this process we see that the banking system creates ten times more in money credits as the original $1000 deposit, increasing the money supply by $10,000. It keeps $1000 in reserve and lends out $10,000, which is represented by deposits in the bank. The bank's accounting balance sheet shows $10,000 in assets (the loans) and $10,000 in liabilities (deposits), only $1000 of which is held in reserve. The 10 to 1 reserve ratio is called the money, or credit, multiplier.

The danger is that, under *abnormal* circumstances, depositors might demand all their money at once, all $10,000, while the bank has only $1000 in its vaults. The loans they extended cannot quickly be recalled. All depositors withdrawing their money at once is called a bank run or panic, and the result is insolvency, or bankruptcy of the bank. Bank runs used to happen frequently during economic downturns, as people grew fearful for their life's savings. Today, the danger of banking panics is mitigated by the Federal Reserve, which provides emergency money as the "lender of last resort." To do this, the Fed merely creates credits and lends them to any bank in need of capital reserves. A federal agency, the Federal Deposit Insurance Corporation (FDIC), also guarantees deposits up to $250,000. The banking system outlined above is called fractional reserve banking. It may sound crazy, and it can be, but not necessarily.

If you think about this illustration deeply enough, you may ask, "Okay, but the first $1000 I deposited came from another transaction and loan. This money creation seems circular. Where does it all start?" It starts with the Federal Reserve System, a consortium of private banks ostensibly under government control, which has the power to create new credits and lend them to the commercial banking system.[22] The Fed does this in several ways (which are not crucial to our discussion), but essentially they lend reserves to commercial banks by crediting their accounts at the Federal Reserve. Banks then commence the credit creation process by making loans to customers. This expands the money supply. The Fed can also reduce the number of loans by calling in these credits, which shrinks the loan portfolios of the banks as they scramble to maintain the 10% capital reserve-to-loan ratio. This contracts the money supply.[23]

The logic of fractional reserve banking is to make the money supply responsive to the demand for money. The demand for money is a function of economic expansion and the need for exchange payments. If the money supply is too tight or fixed, new investment and production is impeded because capital resources must be reallocated from old investments and recycled into new ones. This requires price changes to separate the good investments from the bad. It's a difficult and time-consuming reallocation process. Imagine your loan officer saying, "I'd like to lend you the money, but first I have to recall all these old loans from these deadbeats." The net result of an inelastic currency is slow growth and price deflation. An elastic currency, however, empowers new investment and production. Credit creation is a net positive *IF* the investments made by new loans earn a return sufficient to pay for the loan with additional profit (a big "IF," as we'll see). The management of the money supply through fractional reserve banking is the primary mission of the Federal Reserve.

2.3 Financial Alchemy

Still with us? Please hang in there as we explore the next stage of financial alchemy. If we understand fractional reserve banking, we see that our fiat money supply is *not* actually created by printing presses, but by *credit creation,* denominated in debt outstanding. (When a bank issues a loan, it creates the credit that the borrower assumes as a debt.) It's time to introduce the other major player on the stage: the U.S. Federal government.

Conventionally, the government claims its share of our dollars' value by collecting taxes and using those to pay its (our!) bills. *Or it can borrow.* (This is where the money shell game begins, and the path of the hidden "pea" becomes increasingly hard to follow.)

When the Federal government spends more than it collects in taxes (creating a budget deficit), it borrows the additional money it needs by issuing new Treasury bonds, or debt. The sale and purchase of these bonds soaks up private savings—when you buy a $1000 Treasury bond, you lend your private savings to the government. In return you receive a promise of an interest payment over the life of the bond, and then repayment of the original $1000 principal. The interest rate the government offers depends on the available supply of savings and the buying demand for government bonds. The actual rate is determined by auction – so every couple of weeks the Treasury has a bond sale auction. These bond sales are participated in worldwide; so many buyers are foreigners who exchange the dollars they received for their exports for U.S. government-guaranteed debt. If savings supply or demand is inadequate, the Treasury must raise the interest rate to attract more buyers. Remember, U.S. citizens back up government debt with tax revenues, so technically, taxpayers are the ones who must pay more interest on the borrowing. Some of our fellow citizens will buy the bonds and receive these payments. Other payments will be sent to European or Chinese buyers. The government is constantly issuing new bonds to pay back, or roll over, the maturing principal on bonds issued in past years. In addition, under a fiat currency, the Treasury can just issue new debt to pay that interest, putting the financial reckoning farther off into the future.[24]

So far we have two major players in the credit creation and debt markets—the banking system and the government. The banking system creates credits that are held in the form of private debt (whoever borrows, owes the bank) and the government creates debt through deficit spending in the form of privately held credits (the government owes whoever buys the bonds). The commercial banks' credit creation, under the regulation of the Fed, is what increases or decreases the money supply.

Now, what happens if the Fed buys the government bonds directly from the Treasury? Recall that the Fed has the power to create credit from thin air and can use these credits to buy bonds. Now the Fed holds assets in the form of government bonds. This transaction has two important consequences. Since the Fed provided funds to the Treasury by buying the bonds, private savings were not reduced, but the spending of these credits by the government has increased the supply of money. In addition, these bonds are now reserve assets of the Federal Reserve, increasing the available reserves to the banking system. If the Fed allows commercial banks to borrow these reserves, it increases the supply of credits to the banking system that can be loaned out ten times over to new borrowers.

When the Fed buys bonds directly from the Treasury, we call this "monetizing" the government debt because it *can* drastically increase the money supply.[25] An increase in the money supply has been the traditional source of price inflation, which is just another way of saying the supply of money rises faster than the supply of goods and services it represents, causing all prices to rise. After the 2008 financial crisis, the Fed became a major buyer of Treasury bonds and now holds a greater share of Treasury debt than any other entity— more than $1.2 trillion, roughly 14% of the total Treasury debt outstanding. (China holds $1.1 trillion.)

At this point we might hope that the money supply is somewhat under the control of the Federal Reserve and that the supply can be controlled by virtue of enforcing the right central bank policies. Unfortunately, that's not quite the case. The game gets more complex.

Commercial banks are not the only institutions that lend money. In fact, because banks earn a nice return by extending credit and creating new money backed up by the full faith and credit of the American people, everybody wants to get in on the action. The new players include mortgage lenders, investment banks, large corporations, insurance companies, hedge funds, credit unions; the list goes on. These various players make up what is called the "shadow banking" industry. Supposedly, the U.S. taxpayer is *not* on the hook for the liabilities of these shadow bank credits. *Supposedly.*

After the high inflation of the late 1970s, the Fed turned to these shadow banks to deploy a different strategy for funding the government debt without direct monetization. They encouraged these private financial institutions to buy the debt rather than the commercial banking system. Government debt held by the shadow banking system was used for capital reserves and collateral to create more credit. The excess liquidity poured into financial assets, leading to a sustained boom in stock, bond, and derivatives markets. This strategy enjoyed the advantage of funding the government debt without stoking price inflation in the goods markets.[26] However, this has come at the cost of complicating the Fed's control over the money supply.

The Fed closely regulates commercial banks, while commercial bank deposits are insured by the FDIC. The shadow banking system, however, is outside the regulatory arms of the Fed and mostly subject to regulatory oversight from various other agencies, such as the Securities and Exchange Commission. Foreign financial institutions outside U.S. jurisdiction are completely unregulated by U.S. laws. Thus, the credit controls exercised by the Fed can only weakly constrain the credit creation of the private shadow banking system. The leverage used by shadow banks may far exceed the 10% reserves of the commercial banks, sometimes up to 30 to 40 times. This credit creation takes many forms, from margin debt offered by investment brokers to highly leveraged financial derivatives. For example, you can open a stock brokerage margin account, put in $100,000 in cash, and the brokerage house will allow you to margin that to $200,000 of buying power. They have simply created $100,000 of new credit from nothing, Investment banks increased leverage ratios to create $40 of credits in derivatives for every $1 in capital reserves. This means that a 3% decline in market prices would completely wipe out the bank's equity. This explosion of new credit creation introduced another dangerous wild card into the monetary system.

This discussion of money may be esoteric and somewhat confusing the first time through. The most important fact to understand is that, through the processes outlined above, *the U.S. money supply is wholly based on credit and debt creation that is backed by the full faith and credit of the U.S. government and guaranteed by U.S. taxpayers through the productive capacity of the US economy.* Every dollar of purchasing power represents a debt on which interest is paid to the creditors who created the loans that represent that debt. These creditors include the privately-held Federal Reserve System, all the commercial banks, and the entire shadow-banking system. All these financial institutions are receiving a return by creating money from debt. We can see that the incentive for the bank creditors is to create more money and earn more interest on the debt they issue. This continues until foolish lending turns into bad debt. Then it all comes crashing down. (In Chapter Four we will analyze how this happened in 2008.) In general, the consequence of a credit or debt creation fiat currency system is that nobody has clear control over the money supply. There are few constraints on the system, or even the correct incentives, to ensure a sound monetary system. *The ultimate risk to the US economy, the nation, and its citizens is not the bankruptcy of the government, but the gradual erosion of our standard of living through misguided policies.* This is difficult to understand unless one can see the big picture. It is also much more difficult to discern in short time frames as it is more like the frog being slowly boiled in a pot of water. By the time he realizes it, he's already cooked.

Lastly, we must consider the political interests of the government as the presumed regulator of this system. We know that politicians get elected by promising lower taxes and higher benefits to voters (I address politics in Chapter Three). These political incentives result in deficits funded by excessive government borrowing. The creditors of the fiat currency system, with its incentives to create more debt, have found a ready partner in a government that desires endless borrowing. Eventually, the entire bill must be paid by distracted taxpayers. In simple terms, the financial liability comes down to you and me—only our capability to work will create the necessary wealth to pay back a massive national borrowing spree. Is it any wonder that obfuscation and public confusion favor the architects of this system?

As for the U.S. dollar, *its value has been left to depend on the productive capacity of the U.S. economy, which, in turn, will depend on the successful management of economic policy.* The deeper personal implication is that the ultimate value of your life's hard work, saved as accumulated capital, will depend not only on your own prudent financial judgment, but also on the collective financial behavior of the nation. It's not a comforting thought. (For a flowchart of the credit-debt cycle outlined above see Appendix C.)

2.4 Capital and Financial Markets

Some of the financial assets that trade in world capital markets include stocks (or equities), bonds, commodities, loans, mortgages, real estate trusts, currencies, precious metals, commercial paper, and financial derivatives. New products, which, like those above, help to manage risk and provide capital, are being innovated every day. As this book is not an investment guide, we will not examine these various securities except in terms of how they may affect the macroeconomy. The point I wish to raise here is that these financial asset markets behave differently than the markets for goods and services. To understand this we must first investigate the nature of capital.

The idea of capital is fundamental to understanding our capitalist society. (There's actually a good reason why we call our system *Capitalism* and not *Laborism*.) Many people may think capital is just another name for money, but there are crucial differences. Money, as we mentioned previously, is defined by its three functional uses: as a store of value, a unit of account, and a medium of exchange.

So, what is capital? Capital is any asset—money, land, tools, machinery, knowledge or skill—that is put to work in order to earn a positive return. We can categorize these various forms of capital as financial, physical, human, or social. The important point is that capital at work is capital invested. As such, capital is a crucial ingredient in the production of more goods and services, and yes, in the creation of more capital financially denominated as money. To illustrate the distinction between money and capital we can think of money as a reservoir of water. The water can sit there stagnant, slowly evaporating over time, or it can be fed into a series of irrigation canals, combining with fertilized soil to yield a crop of fruit. Idle money is merely a store of value, but money put to work is financial capital. Combining financial capital with labor, natural resources, and human ingenuity has yielded the vast material wealth of our modern world. Financial capital is an essential ingredient in the production process, and capital markets help to allocate and balance its supply and demand.

The unique quality of financial capital differentiates it from other goods. Financial capital, like money, is only valued when it can be put to work to earn a return. Capital is invested with the anticipation that it will pay back in the form of future streams of income. The right to receive any future stream of income has a certain "capitalized" value called the *fundamental* or *intrinsic* value of capital. We see this most easily in debt instruments that specify the actual cash flows according to the debt contract. A mortgage or a bond are two obvious examples where the present value of future income streams is clearly specified. Other good examples are a utility stock that pays a high dividend, a life insurance annuity, or a house rental payment. A rental apartment has a certain fundamental value that directly relates to the rents paid by the tenant.

As the future is unpredictable, the perceived value of these future income streams can vary considerably. The stream of payments from a Treasury bond with the bond principal amount backed by the U.S. government is considered the most secure of financial assets, so its value is more easily ascertained and relatively stable. Other asset streams, such as high yield corporate bonds (*aka* junk bonds), are much less secure and their bond values can fluctuate widely. Ownership of stock, such as a share of IBM, secures the right to a share of future earnings that may or may not be realized, depending on the success of the business.

As financial asset valuations become more exposed to uncertainty and risk, more of the value is subject to the capricious confidence or uncertainty of market buyers and sellers, and less related to the asset's more stable fundamental value. I may think Ford Motor Company has a bright future, while you believe its prospects look bleak. If some event changes prevailing market opinions one way or the other, the price of Ford stock and its valuation will adjust abruptly. The value of risky capital is thus determined largely by public opinion and is expressed in capital markets that can fluctuate widely from day to day. We will call this the *tradable value* of capital to distinguish it from the *fundamental value* explained above. The price volatility of capital represents an inherent risk because capital value based on emotion can evaporate in an instant. We have all heard the stories of Internet stocks that shot to unrealistic price levels, only to see that valuation vanish completely, and almost immediately, when the euphoric bubble popped. Another way of understanding this is that the value of a financial asset only becomes real when you get that future income flow in your hand.

This subjective, or tradable, value of capital also means that, rather than merely employing capital in production, capital gains and losses can be realized by market traders as valuations fluctuate in price. We all know that perennial investment advice to "buy low and sell high." But for every asset bought at a low price, there was a seller, and for every one sold at a high price there was a buyer. So, trading value is in the eye of the beholder. This causes traders in financial assets to trade based on what *they think others will think*. This becomes a psychological game: I will try to trade by anticipating what you are thinking of doing, and will do my best to influence what you do. The gaming of financial markets creates considerable white noise and uncertainty in the investment world surrounding the valuation of capital. But the problem gets worse.

The demand for financial assets leads to increased prices for those assets. This increased value can then be capitalized into credit that can be used to buy more financial assets. (Like rising housing prices were used to create more lending credit in order to buy more houses and other goods.) The access to credit leverages and amplifies an asset bubble by raising prices of the assets, generating more credit, raising prices again, and so on in a positive feedback loop.

This market process of positive feedback driven by emotion and credit creation is what makes financial markets volatile and unstable. The tradable value of capital thrives on the momentum of emotion that, with credit leverage, can become highly inflated due to what our central bankers have called "irrational exuberance." One economist has referred to the tradable value as the *confidence* value of capital.[27] As confidence in the future increases, the value of capital increases because it can be put to work to create additional wealth. There is a problem, however, in distinguishing justified confidence from false confidence. Most economists agree that asset prices that depart too much from fundamental values are an indication of false confidence (*aka* "pie-in-the-sky" wishful thinking). The tricky part is knowing when they have reached that level.

We can see that financial markets behave very differently from goods markets. For instance, I don't buy a pair of shoes by trying to figure out whether you will pay the same amount, more, or less. I merely decide what the shoes are worth to me and either buy them or not. In goods markets, when the price of a product rises, demand for it goes down, as buyers perceive the price as too rich. When the price of a television doubles, consumer demand for that television falls and the excess inventory forces the producer or retailer to lower the price to the equilibrium point, perhaps with an "inventory sale." As a result of this negative feedback process, supply and demand return to equilibrium. As financial assets increase in price, however, they often become more desirable. As demand increases, financial asset prices rise even higher, *away from an equilibrium based on fundamental values*. This positive feedback process generates a form of herd behavior. As the train is seen leaving the station, investors fear they're missing it and jump on, driving prices into the stratosphere.

As we've observed this phenomenon again and again throughout the history of financial crises, we know only too well what happens next.[28] The tradable value of capital follows what we might call the "bigger fool" theory of investment. An investor overpays for a financial asset in the hope that some "bigger fool" will then buy it from him at an even higher price. There are only so many fools with money to lose in this world. Something always triggers the return of rationality (usually, the easy credit that is fueling such mania dries up) and everyone heads for the exit at once, causing prices to collapse and the bubble to burst. We will discuss the recent housing bubble later, but is this not exactly what happened when we turned houses into get-rich-quick, tradable, financial assets instead of homes? As prices rose, people clamored to jump on board the train before it left the station, driving prices to extraordinary heights. Soon, houses were being bought simply to be "flipped" at a higher price, just like a penny stock. There was even a television show called "Flip This House." Everybody was betting on there being a bigger fool to sell to. There was little relation between home prices and the fundamental values indicated by the incomes of buyers or rental prices of comparable housing.

We can think of capital as the embodiment of confidence in the future and value it accordingly. *Uncertainty* is another concept that is hard to pin down and measure, though we know it when we feel it.[29] It is the opposite of confidence, or "irrational exuberance." When uncertainty increases, the value of capital decreases as the present becomes valued more highly relative to the future. If we knew the world was to end tomorrow, the value of all capital would plunge to zero because it would have no useful value to you over the next 24 hours. Likewise, if we knew we would live forever, capital would be highly valued and in high demand because we would be mindful of what we needed for the future, assured there would be a future, and would save and invest accordingly. This logic explains how the investment banking firm of Bear Stearns could see its capital worth literally evaporate into thin air. As of November 2006, the company had total capital of approximately $66.7 billion and total assets of $350.4 billion. Less than sixteen months later, JP Morgan Chase offered $236 million for the entire firm (later the bid was raised to $1.1 billion). This was a loss of confidence on an epic scale and for Bear Stearns there was no tomorrow.

2.5 Labor and the Problem of Unemployment

Labor utilization and the recurring problem of unemployment have been the major preoccupations of economists since the Great Depression. There are reasons for this that go beyond sympathy for the unemployed. Labor and capital are the primary ingredients to creating wealth. If we have 10% unemployment, then the nation is under producing by at least 10% or more. This adds up to a lot of national income and wealth creation that is lost forever. Of course, since the production process employs both labor and capital, unemployment also means idle capital or capital misallocated toward other, less productive uses, like asset speculation. Full employment and full capacity utilization of available capital has been a primary policy objective for obvious political and economic reasons.

Theories of employment are quite complex and sophisticated, but to simplify them let's refer back to our pie-baking example. Let's assume we have unemployed chefs. One policy solution is to increase the use of capital in combination with more chefs to create more pies. We might encourage this capital utilization by seeking to increase the demand for pies by providing a government subsidy for buying pies (food stamps?). Our solution seems simple: More pie eating leads to higher prices for pies, attracting more capital investment in pie production, which leads to more chefs becoming employed, causing the population to grow fatter and happier. The problem is that the original unemployment may have resulted from some basic behaviors associated with human labor. One is that the price of labor is less flexible than the prices of other goods. If the unemployment is created because wages are too high, the wage will not fall back down to an equilibrium level to realize full employment. Why? Because loss aversion means we are very resistant to reducing our wage incomes. We call this wage rigidity. If wage rigidity is the cause of the original unemployment, trying to artificially stimulate the demand for pies to employ more chefs at the prevailing wage is the wrong policy because it is unsustainable. The government subsidies will need to go on forever, and it might be more economical just to give the subsidies directly to the unemployed chefs to retrain for another job. In our example, if there are too many unemployed chefs, perhaps chefs are commanding salaries that are too high given the demand for pies and the revenues of the bakery. But how do we get a chef to reduce his/her wage or perceived value? Unfortunately, this can usually be achieved only through layoffs and unemployment, which is the problem we were seeking a solution for in the first place. This conundrum is evidence of a market failure.

Another problem with unemployment is that it is difficult for available labor to find the proper match with capital. There are considerable search costs and mobility problems for job and career changes. If one lives in California and the baking jobs are in Texas or Florida, it is quite costly to pack up the family and move. (The housing crisis we engineered over the past decade will only further increase this relative immobility and misallocation of labor, as people cannot afford to absorb large losses on the sales of their existing homes.) So, the impediment of search costs represents another potential labor market failure.

The policy problem we face is how to overcome these market failures and match up capital with labor to increase production. It is not a simple task and is fraught with intellectual controversy.

2.6 Competing Macroeconomic Theories

There are several competing schools of thought on macroeconomic policy, each with various offshoots. We shall discuss the two most dominant ones: the Keynesian and Classical schools. Both theoretical approaches must choose from the same selection of fiscal and monetary policy tools, which have traditionally focused on the interest rate, taxes, and government spending. Recently, the monetary authorities have introduced some new policy tools that encompass direct loans, guarantees, and asset purchases (the infamous bailouts and 'quantitative easing" QE1, QE2, etc. – all of these basically increase liquidity, i.e. inject cash, into the banking system to shore up the financial sector of the economy.)

We'll begin our discussion with the interest rate, since that is fundamental to our market model. As we've discussed, economic decisions over time are guided by the interest rate, which helps to balance the supply and demand for capital and to balance consumption and savings over time. During a growth cycle, when confidence in the future is high, interest rates will rise and present consumption will be deferred as investment is increased. Savings will rise to supply credit for additional investment demand as opportunities warrant. Production increases. In boom times we borrow from future consumption, confident that we will have greater income in the future to pay loans back without reducing future consumption. In short, the pie is growing; so all the pieces get bigger. Most recently, this scenario unfolded in the U.S. during the 1990s technology boom.

On the downside, when the future becomes more uncertain, the value of capital falls and interest rates decline. The pie is now shrinking as income, consumption, and savings all decline. The desire to save increases due to uncertainty, but low interest rates do not adequately increase present consumption demand or new investment. As production declines, the lack of investment demand will keep interest rates low and borrowing will likely be channeled into bidding up real asset or commodity prices. The resulting asset bubbles foreshadow the contraction phase of the economic cycle, which then causes these same asset prices to collapse. We have been experiencing this phase of the economic cycle off and on since 2001. The Zero Interest Rate Policy (ZIRP) the Fed has conducted since the 2008 financial crisis is reflected in the low interest on savings, sputtering demand, and increases in commodity prices such as food and energy.

In our model the interest rate is a price signal that reflects the overall desire to consume or save, and the incentives to invest and produce. The interest rate will reflect economic fundamentals, such as technology cycles and demographics, and also the short term effects of policy and financial market confidence or uncertainty. Because of its critical role in the allocation of capital, the interest rate is the most important price to get right. Fortunately, or perhaps unfortunately, the interest rate is also the most accessible tool the Federal Reserve can manipulate to affect the economy.[30]

As we have shown with our simple model and the discussion of capital and labor markets, the macroeconomy can become unstable due to human nature and the dynamics of financial markets. During a growth cycle, the feedback from financial markets tends to encourage *overinvestment* relative to present and future consumption. The result is too much capital chasing fewer and fewer productive investments, until the investments eventually result in negative, rather than positive, returns. The decline in the value of capital leads to an economic contraction, or what we would commonly call a recession or depression.

After the Great Depression of the 1930s, policymakers under the influence of the renowned economist John Maynard Keynes began to recognize the problem of inadequate private consumption demand over time. Inadequate consumption leads to less investment and lower production, which, in a vicious cycle, lead to even less consumption demand. Fiscal policies were formulated to stimulate demand, leading to government spending that supplemented the private economy. These programs included temporary measures, such as the Works Progress Administration under the New Deal, and more lasting ones such as national unemployment insurance and Social Security. Under certain conditions, such government spending can work very well. However, one of the problems that arises when the economy gets off-track is that price signals get distorted. Government stimulus can often perpetuate, if not exacerbate, these price distortions, sending more wrong market signals and reducing efficiency.

In response, Classical theorists, or market fundamentalists, argue that getting prices right and reallocating resources, especially capital and labor, is essential to righting the economy and getting it back on a growth path. Politically motivated government spending is likely to only make matters worse. But a correction of distorted market prices often means certain asset prices and certain labor costs must adjust downward. This implies business losses and rising unemployment, which are usually politically untenable. There is no clean reconciliation of these two approaches. It is more a matter of which approach one chooses to favor under any given economic circumstance.

The primary fiscal tools available to policymakers are tax policy and public spending programs. Classicalists favor cutting taxes to encourage private sector investment and reducing the dead-weight costs of public sector spending, while Keynesians favor increased government spending and public investment to stimulate present consumption and production. The tug of war between these competing visions, over the last three decades especially, has given us tax cuts *plus* spending increases, with the result that the gap between them is funded by an exploding level of public debt. This has landed us where we are now. Our focus should not be on the *level of debt* as much as on measuring what this debt accumulation is doing for us – is it making us more productive and richer, or less so?

Another serious problem we face today is that the feedback signals from the macroeconomy have become deliberately distorted. We hear various statistics announced every week in the media. The three main ones that capture our politicians' attentions are Gross Domestic Product (GDP), the unemployment rate, and the Consumer Price Index (CPI). All three statistics have been manipulated in recent years with new formulas that bias the information they were designed to convey. For instance, core CPI inflation statistics, which determine wage and Social Security cost of living adjustments (COLAs), do not include food and energy price changes, even though these have a big impact on household spending patterns and also. Then, in 1983, housing price changes were removed from the index, further understating one of the largest costs facing families, especially in the last ten years. A widely subscribed alternate statistical service estimates that our current level of inflation as of early 2011 is closer to 10% than the reported CPI of 1%, and that our meaningful unemployment level is closer to 23% than the reported 9.4%. Our real GDP is -2% rather than the reported 3.4%.[31] The biases also indicate some conflicts of interest among those who determine these statistics. A lower reported CPI allows the government to pay out less in benefits and inflation-adjusted bonds because these payments are keyed off the CPI. We have already discussed how confidence has a real impact on the valuation of capital, so this strategy on the part of our political leaders to overstate the "good news" is not surprising. Ultimately, however, the data we use to formulate policy are misleading and have been corrupted by politics.

Given the distortions in the statistics our policymakers use to measure macroeconomic performance (GDP, the unemployment rate, CPI), it is little wonder that their preferred solution to every problem is to maximize real GDP growth to make all these statistics look better. This is also where our current macroeconomic theories and tools gain the most traction with their proposed solutions. It's a little bit like the old saying that if you only have a hammer, every problem looks like a nail. Economic growth has become the solution for every problem. We can agree that growth is a good measure of material well-being and brings improvements in the quality of life. But, as we have demonstrated with our simple model of sustainable growth, the economy is a system of flows between consumption, saving, investment, and production over time. This system of flows is a *distributional* process. Sustainable economic growth is a function of how we *distribute* or *allocate* our resources across different activities over time. So while politicians and economists have been focusing on the *production* problem—how to produce more—ultimately, we must also face the distributional problem, for which we have few solid answers.

Imagine we have a field of crops that we need to fertilize and water. If our irrigation system delivers all the water to only one half of the field and we spread all our fertilizer on the other half, or if we fertilize this month and water next month, is there any doubt our crop yield is likely to be dismal? It is essential that the water and fertilizer be efficiently and adequately distributed in proper proportions across the entire field. This is also true for the distribution of capital and labor in our economic production process. Distributional allocations across the entire economy over how much to produce must sync with the consumption demand for specific products between now and the future. We need to sprinkle our capital, labor, energy and others resources in the right proportions across the economy. You can imagine the difficulty of getting this right because the objective is dependent on getting hundreds of millions of people to do what is necessary, and to do so voluntarily. If we get the policies wrong, say, by encouraging everyone to speculate in trading houses, then the economy will list and capsize like a boat where all the passengers run to one side. In 2008/9 the world economy actually did capsize. Now it is struggling to right itself, but the problems that swamped it remain.

2.7 Distributional Failures

I like to make the argument that our most challenging economic problems are problems of maldistributions, or skewed distributions, of essential resources. In economics these are sometimes referred to as coordination failures, but I prefer distributional failures. At a recent social gathering among friends I noted an amusing anecdote to illustrate the issue.

Several of us folically-challenged men were being teased as being "bald." One friend came to my rescue, grabbing the shock of hair at the back of my head to claim, "Look, he has lots of hair." I readily seconded him by explaining that I did not have a "balding" problem, I had sprouted lots of new hair in recent years – on my back, in my nose, out my ears – the real problem was that it was all in the wrong places. It was the *maldistribution* of hair! Mine is not a problem of baldness, but male pattern thinning (and that can be fixed). A bald man needs a miracle cure to promote new hair growth, but a man with pattern baldness merely needs a good transplant surgeon.

The problem of market distribution is much the same and the cure must also be correctly tailored to the problem. For example, we know how to grow enough food and create enough wealth in this world, but we haven't really figured out how to distribute that food and wealth to the most needy, whether they are living in inner-city America or in some impoverished African nation. Clean water and medicine also present failures of distribution; education and investment in human capital also requires getting the goods to the people who will employ them.

But distributional failures are more than a matter of delivery; the problem is more a matter of the neediest having the means to create the wealth necessary to pay for the good *and* its delivery. In macroeconomics, the problem we've discovered in business cycles is that demand is not distributed adequately across the population over time. This becomes reflected in levels of investment and production. Every week we can read new reports in the media on the growing gaps in wages, income, and wealth. The skewed distribution of the means of producing wealth (financial and human capital) is probably the most critical and intractable economic problem we face and one we need to solve. I contend that this is more than a social or political problem; it is a macroeconomic problem that will require appropriate economic policies. Our flow system of economic production and exchange is constrained by growing inequality. These distributional failures become even more challenging when we realize we are dealing with the world economy rather than just the U.S. national economy.

2.8 Globalization: National vs. International Economy

We have been treating the U.S. macroeconomy as if it was a closed system, where all inputs and outputs must balance over time. This is similar to looking at the earth as a closed system where we must recycle energy and resources in order to sustain life. (Of course, the earth ultimately receives all its energy from the sun, which the physicists say will burn out someday as the universe expands, but let's not go there.) The international global economy *is* a closed system. We don't trade with Martians or get financed by aliens—all trade among earthlings is conducted in a closed system. However, each sovereign nation has a domestic economy that is not a closed system, but is part of an open, global international system of trade and capital exchange markets.

Within the global system, each sovereign nation controls its own macroeconomic policies, which differ from nation to nation. Thus, the imbalances we have been discussing that can lead to market failures and economic crises can be complicated by imbalances among national economies and national policies. The best illustration is the contrast between China and the United States over the past two decades. China has been saving, producing, and exporting while the U.S. has been borrowing and spending on consumption. This behavior on a national scale leads to imbalances in consumption, saving, investing and production between the two countries that are often aggravated by policies. Without overcomplicating the problem, we should understand that one country cannot only sell while another one only buys. Imagine if you traded with your neighbor, selling things, but never buying anything in return. Soon you would have all his money and he would have all your goods. Then you lend him money to buy even more goods that you could make and sell. But he'd never be able to pay you back. Imagine this type of exchange between countries and you will understand some of the irrationality of the international system. Sovereign nations that wish to increase their national wealth pursue policies that subsidize the export, or selling, sector. But every nation cannot be a net exporter, unless we're also selling to Martians and other non-earthlings.

Currency exchange rates[32] can unduly complicate our intuitive model of the international economy, but a basic understanding of them is necessary. We have discussed how price signals, such as the price of money (the interest rate), affect our economic choices. The exchange rate between one nation's currency and another's affects all prices between these two nations uniformly. If the U.S. dollar's value relative to the euro falls by 50%, then all goods and services that Americans can buy from Europeans will be twice as expensive in dollar prices, while all the goods and services that Europeans buy from Americans will be halved in euro prices. This means U.S. exports will be much cheaper for Europeans and Europeans exports to the U.S. will be much more expensive. This will cause U.S. consumers to cut back on European goods and substitute U.S. goods, and also cause U.S. exporters to increase production to sell to Europeans. The net national effect will be to shift Americans to saving and producing more and to shift Europeans into buying and consuming more while saving and producing less. We can apply this logic to the imbalance between the U.S. and China noted above. Because of the imbalances between Chinese and U.S. consumption patterns, the Chinese currency should appreciate relative to the dollar, causing Americans to produce more for export and Chinese consumers to consume more American exports. Unfortunately, national governments often interfere with market rebalancing of exchange rates for political reasons. They may adopt economic policies that keep the national currency undervalued in order to promote export production. With exchange rates out of whack, trade imbalances grow.

National economic policies diverge because of political demands from citizens and the need for politicians to meet those demands in order to win elections, or, in the case of non-democracies, to stay in power. Most populations consistently want a better, higher quality of life, which is measured by rising GDP. This also means they desire a more competitive claim on the world's resources such as food, energy, labor, and capital, which puts them in competition with other nations. Policies that seek to maximize wealth by attracting the necessary resources for production run into a problem because of the *mobility of capital relative to labor*. What this means is that one can send one's capital in an instant to any part of the world for investment. But a nation's labor resources must rely on migration or immigration to relocate, so the ideal combination of capital and labor is difficult to engineer. We see the side effects of this in the dislocations caused by outsourcing and illegal immigration as capital flows to where labor is cheapest and surplus labor tries to migrate to nations with scarcer, higher paid, labor. While the reallocation of capital and labor helps to increase wealth in a closed world economy, the process entails high social and economic costs, such as those borne by workers who get displaced. This creates more demands from domestic groups for trade protection, as well as what we call "beggar thy neighbor" economic policies, to resist globalization. The term was originally devised to characterize policies of trying to cure domestic depression and unemployment by shifting effective demand away from imports onto domestically produced goods, either through tariffs, quotas on imports, or by competitive devaluation. This last strategy, to manipulate the currency either to attract more capital or increase exports by making them cheaper, offers a solution that is often worse than the disease because unstable currency values inhibit productive investment.

For a stable world economy, which for all practical purposes is a closed economic system, we need national economies to be more self-sustaining over time. Properly managed through national economic policies, globalization's benefits can far outweigh its costs. Producing/exporting countries will have to consume more, and consuming/importing countries will have to save, invest, and produce more. But national economic policies that are responding to the demands of competing populations are extremely difficult to coordinate. This political dilemma contributed to the international trade protectionism that exacerbated the Great Depression. It's not possible for all of us to be richer than our neighbors, but since wealth is the source of power and material freedom, the competitive desire to surpass our fellows will not soon disappear. (Nor, necessarily, should it.)

2.9 Risk, Uncertainty, and Insurance

Since we live in a world of constant change and the effects of change are unpredictable, we are always operating in an environment of risk and uncertainty. It is the nature of our world. One of my favorite quotes on uncertainty was given by Donald Rumsfeld in a speech in 2002, when he was Secretary of Defense:

> ...as we know, there are known knowns; there are things we know we know. We also know there are known unknowns; that is to say we know there are some things we do not know. But there are also unknown unknowns -- the ones we don't know we don't know. And if one looks throughout the history of our country and other free countries, it is the latter category that tend to be the difficult ones.

The wisdom of Secretary Rumsfeld's remarks on "unknown unknowns" have been underappreciated by the chattering classes ever since, who found amusement in his exposition (see "*unks-unks*.") But such uncertainties, whose unpredictability we cannot touch or grasp, operate in the recesses of our mind and have profound implications for our choices in life.

I find risk and uncertainty to be the most fascinating topic in political economy. I also believe it is the most important concept—the key—to understanding our economic and political environment. As we are living organisms operating under the imperative to survive and reproduce, nature has made us most sensitive to risks to our survival, whether we are aware of this fact or not. We act on our survival instinct without thinking, just like any other sentient being. This means that the risks we perceive in our everyday environment will impact significantly on our behavior.

The best demonstration for me of how the fear instinct dominates our innate behavior was when I went up the CN Tower in Toronto. At the top there was a large section of the flooring constructed with thick, see-through glass. Through the glass one could see straight down to the ground, more than one thousand feet down. It was fascinating to observe, but I found that I could not walk out over the glass floor. My rational mind knew there was no possibility the glass could break, but still, my survival instinct overpowered any rational thought. Try it some time. My bodily reaction confirms a wealth of behavioral studies that support the conclusion that our risk-taking choices are determined not by the question: "What will I gain?" but by the question: "What do I have to lose?"

As our universe is uncertain, and our human nature is driven by loss aversion, the concepts of risk and uncertainty connect our individual selves with the broader universe, admittedly in a non-spiritual, material sense. If we can get a handle on how the uncertainties of our changing environment shape our perceptions of risk, we will have a powerful analytical tool that can help us understand human behavior and social science phenomena.

Let us take, for example, the historical development of large scale business enterprise. Big business needs adequate capital to fund its investment projects, but early on there were few sources of capital that would willingly assume such risks at a price any one enterprise could afford to pay. The later development of joint-stock ownership allowed investors to spread their risks across different capital investments, thus reducing the returns investors would demand from a single enterprise, thereby lowering the cost of capital to that enterprise. The joint-stock company was first adopted by the East India Company in order to expand its international shipping trade in the 17th century, though there are cases of shared risk enterprises going back to Roman days. The modern public corporation added to the diversified risk model with a legal design that provides limited liability for the corporation's owners (i.e., stockholders). This limits the risks of new investment to the assets of the corporation, not to the assets of its owners. When you buy a share of IBM, the most you can lose is the value of that share—i.e., nobody who has a claim against IBM can go after your house or your car. This sharing of risk through capital markets reduces the cost of capital (because more investors are willing to provide the firm with more capital, the price of this capital goes down) and promotes risk-taking investment. The merchants of risk—those bankers and traders on Wall Street and other financial centers across the globe—have developed a wide variety of financial product innovations that include bonds, equities, and a mind-boggling array of financial derivatives. These markets promote risk-taking enterprise and allow anyone who wishes to share in successful enterprise to invest according to their risk preferences. If we think iPods and iPhones are great products, we can choose to invest in Apple and share in the wealth created.

The importance of risk has become more apparent after our recent financial debacle, which most people now understand resulted from a colossal disregard for risk and the theory of risk management. The biggest impact was in the financial sector because the financial sector's *raison d'être* is risk management. "Systemic risk" and "too big to fail" have now become part of the popular vernacular; unfortunately, we learned the consequences after the fact.

From an analytical point of view, risk and uncertainty are not exactly the same thing. Uncertainty is like not knowing which horse will win at the track, or even if the race will run or the weather will hold. Risk enters when we've placed a bet on a particular horse, a bet with real money that we may lose. Exposure to risk is not just borne by money or capital. It is also present, for instance, for the jockey who may fall off the horse and suffer serious injury. We place the bet and the jockey runs the race because we both hope to gain from a successful wager.[33]

There are several important insights we need to understand about risk and uncertainty. The first is that the risks associated with uncertainty are ubiquitous. We cannot eliminate the risk of life in this uncertain world. We can only manage it. Because we are loss averse, our incentive is always to reduce our risk exposure (*all other things being equal*). We can increase our risk exposure, and we often do so in search of higher rewards (like the bettor or the jockey in our example), but we cannot eliminate the fundamental risks of an uncertain existence. Accidents do and will happen. We have little control over whether our industry succeeds, allowing us to keep our jobs. Our attempts to avoid these risks usually only shift those risks onto someone else (see explanation below).

The second insight is that there is only one way to manage uncertainty. This is demonstrated by nature through diversity and diversification. Diversification is the survival imperative of biology. Similarly, we humans diversify with our skills, education, and also with our asset portfolios. This is why financial advisors tell us not to "put all our eggs in one basket."

The science of risk is based on the theory of probability. We can calculate probabilities of chance that allow us to price the risk of loss and then pool together independent events to protect us against possible loss. This is the logic of the insurance industry. We pay insurers a premium based on the small probability of loss, like a house fire or accident, which only pays off if we suffer the loss. The insurance pools all these premiums based on the probability of an event occurring and charges enough to cover the losses and yet still allow for a profit. Since one house burning will not likely cause other houses to burn, the events are independent and the insurance company will use the premiums of all the insured to pay off the loss of the one. (They also invest premiums and realize returns before they ever have to pay out, which helps them enhance their profits and keep premiums down.)

We can also manage our risk exposure by *hedging*, counterbalancing one risky gamble with another that will pay off if we lose the first. This is really just another form of diversification, as it seeks two actions that respond to events in opposite ways. This is a common financial strategy that has given its name to an entire industry.

Diversification is the foundation of portfolio theory that we employ for pension and retirement funds. While we may diversify our human capital by acquiring skills and education, it is much more effective to manage unknown risks by accumulating diversified real and financial assets, such as houses, fine art and collectibles, precious metals, and financial assets that are spread geographically and also across industry sectors. The explosion of financial markets around the world and the innovations in financial instruments has now made this diversification possible for the average citizen investor.[34]

It is important to note, as stated above, that the diversification model only works if contingent events are independent. Dependent events, such as a hurricane or an earthquake, which hits all the houses in a neighborhood at once, create major losses for insurance diversification models. This is why it is often too costly to buy such insurance if, and where, you need it. More seriously, the interdependence of world financial markets has impeded diversification efforts. The risks associated with financial contagion are increased when all financial markets collapse at the same time. Incomplete insurance markets have been served by government-directed social insurance programs like Social Security, Medicare, and unemployment and disability insurance. More on these later.

The efficacy of insurance also depends on the behavior of the insured. If auto insurance causes a driver to drive more recklessly, then the insurer's calculation of the risk probabilities will be wrong, leading to losses for the insurer. This is called <u>moral hazard,</u> and can be a costly problem for insurance. Moral hazard also afflicts social insurance. Social Security can cause people to save less for retirement, or subsidized health care may cause people to be more cavalier with their health.

Our third insight is that risk is a negative good (i.e. we will pay someone to take it away from us). For someone to buy that risk there must exist the promise of a possible return (we don't bet on horses if there is no possibility of winning). So when risks are shifted from one party to another, say from you to the insurance company, the payment of a return associated with that risk (the annual insurance premium) goes with it. This return-risk relationship is the first law of finance: the higher the risk taken, the higher the reward (or the potential loss). The lower the risk, the lower the potential reward or the potential loss. This is called the *reward-to-risk ratio*, or the risk-adjusted rate of return. It's not difficult to observe this relationship in almost every risk-taking decision we make. As with our previous analogy of the roulette table, the tendency toward equalizing the reward-to-risk ratio operates the same way in the economy. Facing different risky choices, we choose the one with the higher reward-to-risk ratio. More accurately stated: because the outcome is uncertain and we are loss averse, we choose the level of risk we are comfortable with first, and then choose the strategy with the highest possible expected reward. The demand for this choice drives the price up, bringing the reward-to-risk ratio down into line with all other options.[35]

As humans hate the risks associated with losses, but crave the gains, the incentive for all players is to secure the gains, while shifting the risks to someone else. However, these outcomes violate the accepted moral rules governing risk-taking behavior, which is that each person bear the consequences of his/her action. Many bankers, politicians, CEOs, and public unions have gotten away with the crime of "heads we win, tails you lose" in recent years by using the taxpayer as a guarantor of risk. This is what we call "socializing the risk and privatizing the gain." It is in the interest of moral and legal justice to prevent this type of behavior and we can find support in legal statutes that defend the innocent from the crimes of the guilty.

One of the more contentious cases of socializing risk and privatizing gain has been the case of public union contracts that secure higher wages and benefits from politicians in return for political support. Public unions have insulated themselves from economic risk by assigning this risk to the taxpayers. Solutions should not focus on what these public service employees deserve or need, but whether the contracts are financially sound and fair given the uncertainty of the economic climate. Obviously, judging from the debt crises afflicting many of the states, they are not financially sound. Now it is becoming clear that those footing the bill—the taxpayers—were not satisfactorily represented at the bargaining table, and because these contracts represent binding legal commitments that states cannot abrogate through bankruptcy, resolving this unsustainable situation will invite political conflict and crisis.

The fourth and final insight flows from the reward-to-risk ratio. Since reward follows risk, or should, we can comprehend how the wealth of rewards gets distributed across society by understanding how risks are shared and borne. The distribution of risk-bearing reveals the just distribution of rewards. An interesting illustration of this is the case of Warren Buffett, considered the richest and most successful investor in America, if not the world. Buffett based his investment strategy on buying up calculated risks and then collecting the rewards for successfully managing those risks. His primary investment vehicle has always been reinsurance, so Buffett's company (Berkshire Hathaway) assumes insurance risk, gets paid for it, then reinvests the premiums in a larger portfolio of business assets on which additional profits are made.

Since all investment in the future is a form of risk-taking, by noting who bears the risks, we can be fairly confident of knowing how the rewards of economic success will be distributed. The insight that risk demands reward and reward entails risk is especially critical to policy.

Before moving on let us summarize these four insights:

1. Risk and uncertainty are ubiquitous
2. We manage the risks of uncertainty through diversification
3. Risk-bearing demands a reward
4. The distribution of risk has a direct relationship to the distribution of reward.

In this chapter we took the simple model of the macroeconomy introduced in Chapter One and examined how the model works in a dynamic setting over time. Since the workings of the economy are quite complex, it may help to review the ideas introduced before continuing to the next chapter on politics.

First, the macroeconomy needs to find a balance among the various activities that make up its whole: consumption, saving, investment and production. Markets are important tools that facilitate this balancing process.

Nevertheless, for a variety of reasons markets can and do fail. The challenge then is to use our knowledge to get the economy back on track.

We must understand the functioning of the capital markets and how they impact the real economy, either by helping it expand or by destabilizing it with recurring financial crises. This ability is mostly due to the unique nature of financial assets as compared to other goods or service markets. The value of capital is highly vulnerable to subjective judgments of the future, falling with uncertainty and rising with confidence.

Sustainable economic growth results from the efficient allocation of capital and labor employed in production. A major complication is combining labor with capital so that the economy fully utilizes the supply of labor. Unemployment has become an important political, as well as economic issue.

Unfortunately, there is no firm consensus on which policies can best return the economy to an equilibrium growth path, so there is much disagreement between different schools of thought. There are also problems with how we measure economic performance as statistics like GDP, inflation and unemployment have been manipulated.

Merely increasing production and economic growth is not a panacea for all our economic ills. The problem is not so much producing more, but in achieving a stable and sustainable path of economic growth over time. The difficulties we face are distributional in nature and require the ability to analyze feedback processes in the economy. We also need to manage the imbalances of flows between nations that are responding to their own political demands with policies that conflict with our own.

The final complication is that we operate in an environment of risk and uncertainty. Both the reality and the perception of this environment have important consequences for the design of various economic policies and their successful outcomes.

In the next chapter we will examine how the democratic political process in its various dimensions—including electoral politics, parties, voters and the media—helps shape the policymaking arena.

CHAPTER THREE

The Politics of Policy

Understanding the political process is essential to comprehending the macroeconomy and the real world environment in which policy is enacted. Dysfunctional politics not only lead to the wrong policies, but also inhibit the political will to make policy changes or reforms before problems lead to crises. As with economics, the critical issues in politics revolve around change and the adaptation to change. In fact, we'll find that the electoral and governing structures of American politics can impede pre-emptive change and that radical but necessary policy reforms are inevitably crisis-driven. Nevertheless, we should recognize that resistance to change is often the trade-off for a measure of political stability.

American politics has become cranky and cantankerous in recent years. Perhaps it started with the Johnson presidency and the divisions of the Vietnam War that shaped a generation. Our divisiveness was amplified by Nixon's transgressions and became hardened during the Reagan-Bush-Clinton eras. Partisan polarization finally began to rule the day when the 2000 election was decided by the Supreme Court in favor of George W. Bush. This caused a large proportion of the voting public to question the legitimacy of the presidency. The war in Iraq did nothing to dampen our differences. Despite all the hopes and promises, the Obama era has failed to bridge this divide and the administration's first two years have probably aggravated our political divisions. Hence we now have the Tea Party, a grassroots movement that demands fealty from both parties, and the recent historic repudiation of a president who rode to victory on a tide of good will. What do we make of all this? Unfortunately, our media outlets have largely joined the fray and politicized their reporting of the facts, leading to widespread distrust of politically-charged information. While democracy does not depend on us all being well-informed, it is certainly hampered by most of us being misinformed.

3.1 Democracy and the Two-Party System

One rudimentary problem that hinders our political discussions is that many of us have an unclear idea on what democracy is and how our particular American form of democracy works. The word *democracy* comes from Greek and means "rule of the people." That idea has been transformed in various ways into a political form of government where governing power is derived from the people by consensus, by direct referendum, or by means of elected representatives of the people. The U.S. chose this last means of divining the will of the people through *representative* democracy. We should note here that the formal definition of democracy does not specify "one person, one vote" or "majority rule." These terms are characteristic of voting rules or *how* we arrive at a social choice, but they are often confused with the principles of democratic "rule of the people." Ours is a representative democracy, or democratic republic, constrained by a formal written constitution enumerating state and federal powers, individual rights, and establishing the checks and balances of the three branches of government.

Arguments claiming how the U.S. Senate or Electoral College are "undemocratic," merely because they are not based on majority rule, are confused or misstated. The Senate is one of the three branches of balanced government and the Electoral College is an institution that helps determine how we select a president through election rules. As parts of our governing system, neither violate the idea or spirit of democracy. To clear up this confusion this we need to separate the electoral system as a way to 'determine the will' of the people, from the process of 'governing' a free people. The former is the voting method by which we the citizenry make social choices; the second is the institutional structure of enacting and executing those choices. In other words, we need to distinguish between *voting* and *governing*.

There are many different voting systems we can apply to determine the public will. There is rule of the simple majority, the supermajority, plurality, proportional representation, instant runoff, weighted or cumulative voting, among others. This is not the place to discuss these varying methods, but the main point is that each of these methods biases different outcomes and these biases impose trade-offs. Unfortunately, there is no God-given, perfect method to enumerate and aggregate all the individual preferences of the mass of voters to come up with a single perfect social choice.[36] Voting "rules" are not a fixed principle of democracy, they are merely various social choice mechanisms where we must choose between competing visions. The *democratic* principle is the "right" to participate in that choice through universal suffrage. Thus, when we compare voting methods we must decide first what the objective is (Make everybody happy? Make everybody free? Make everybody equal?), and then discover how different methods weight these objectives. Again, there is no perfect solution and I will constrain this discussion to the pros and cons of the system we have chosen in the United

States.

The U.S. voting system for state and federal offices is based on the plurality rule, where the candidate that gets the most votes wins. As we also have single-member electoral districts we refer to our method as single-member district plurality (SMDP). This method favors a two-party system since the candidate that gets closest to or beyond the 50% threshold will be the winner. However, plurality voting also means that with three or more candidates, the winning candidate may win with a minority of the total votes cast. For example, if candidates A, B, & C respectively win 30%-30%-40% of the vote, then candidate C wins with 40% of the total. So 60% of the polity is unsatisfied with the result. But candidates A & B could have formed a party coalition and won with 60% of the vote. Party organizations and voters realize this and strategize to capture 50% or more of the vote. This is why third party movements in American politics are rarely successful over time. The third party either displaces or is absorbed by one of the two major parties, or withers away from lack of support. Our SMDP electoral system is deliberate and is the reason we have a two-party system in American politics.

Is this a bad thing or a good thing? Many Americans argue that we should have proportional representation (PR) and multiple member districts where all voting preferences receive representation in proportion to their voting support. So, if a party gets 20% of the vote they get one-fifth of the seats representing that constituent district. But what would be the likely result? Would we have better democracy? Certainly we would have something different. A two-party system forces people to come to the center of compromise in order to win elections. This forces voters to prioritize their preferences and find common political goals. A multiparty system with PR allows different groups to maintain their preferences and refuse compromise, yet still maintain influence in government. In Europe we see this with many different parties with incompatible political agendas. Their governing coalitions include a garden variety of Greens, Socialists, Liberals, Conservative, Social Democrats, even Communists. The main difference is that the American system forces compromise with the penalty of exclusion for uncompromising positions, while the European system allows wider inclusion with the penalty of unstable governing coalitions and inconsistent policies. So, are Europeans happier? Better governed? Richer or more equal? More politically stable? The objectives and priorities of governing—freedom, happiness, equality, inclusion, stability—shape the answers to these questions.

The United States is a geographically large country with an ethnically and racially diverse population. It seems wise to force these various constituencies towards common centrist political objectives so that our governing compromises are more efficient and fair. Successful European countries are much smaller and far more homogenous in their populations. These differences of geography and size and diversity are not trivial. In fact, we will discover how geography, along with associated lifestyle choices and ideologies, has been the most significant factor shaping American party politics over our 200+ year history.

3.2 Federalism

The United States of America is a federation made up of the "several" states. Note that we did not call our country The *Nation* of America; we call it the *United States* of America. Citizens hold a U.S.A passport, but we vote, pay taxes, and claim residency by state. This has important implications for how we govern ourselves. The U.S. is politically divided into geographic constituencies: states, counties, Congressional districts, and municipalities. As you know, we have fifty states and 535 congressional districts, but also approximately 3,143 counties, and an estimated 18,000+ separate municipalities. We administer our government through these various constituent entities. What this offers is a wide diversity of self-determination through the political process. Thus, New Yorkers can choose different policies than Texans, Montanans can choose differently than Californians, and Floridians can choose differently than Washingtonians. Both the U.S. Constitution and fifty state constitutions also mandate how the functions of government are distributed among Federal, state, county, and municipal jurisdictions.

What this means is that our Federal republic affords democracy many laboratories of different constituencies for politics and policy. As with economics, we have political *markets* with feedback mechanisms. These different constituencies not only give us a wide choice of where and how we wish to live, they offer a dynamic, diversified market for testing new ideas for policy and self-government. More important, federalism defends individual liberties by denying any one government entity complete jurisdiction over public life. One can appeal to local, state, or Federal governments in order to defend one's rights. In these many respects, federalism affords our democracy a political fluidity and adaptability that no centralized, hierarchical government could ever match. I doubt very much we would ever choose to give up such governing flexibility.

Our federal system of representative democracy does not contradict the fact that certain functions of government must be carried out at the federal level. Our constitution enumerates these various powers. We do not have fifty different currencies, but one. We do not have fifty different foreign policies, but one (hopefully). The constitutional debates we have are often over which policy jurisdictions should be assigned to a Federal government in Washington D.C. and which should be reserved for states or counties. These debates inform our discussions over whether national policies should take command over such issues as education, health care, or entitlements.

3.3 Politics and Policy

Let's return to our discussion of electoral politics and policymaking. Because elections are won by appealing to a simple majority (50% + 1), or plurality (the most votes), of the voters, successful candidates will be driven toward a centrist position on most issues. This would appear to be the most promising locale for consensus and compromise that would attract the most voting support. Winning the center is the rationale for party organizing, conventions, and election platforms. The idea is to attract a majority of votes in national elections in order to obtain what politicians call a "mandate" for change. This "mandate" is seen as a requirement to overcome the deliberate inertia of the national legislative process.

Our national legislative process is characterized by checks and balances among three branches of government. Policy ideas are often proposed during campaigns by the executive branch or by legislators, and are then formulated in the legislature, or Houses of Congress, made up of the House of Representatives and the Senate. To become law, a bill must pass by a simple majority in both the House and the Senate. Different amended versions are reconciled and voted on. (A *filibuster* is the procedure whereby forty or more Senators can block a vote by preventing cloture on the floor debate of that legislation, effectively killing the bill.) Bills that pass both Houses of Congress must then be signed by the president to become law. A presidential veto can only be overturned by a two-thirds majority in both Houses of Congress.

The law must then survive any legal challenges that are filed and brought up before the judiciary. In other words, an "unconstitutional" action that becomes law must be struck down by a court action filed by an aggrieved party. If not, it will stand until it is challenged.

We can easily see how procedural rules in the legislative process are stacked in favor of the status quo. A high level of consensus is needed to achieve anything, and many roadblocks can be erected to derail bills before becoming law. The process is intentionally conservative in order to make change difficult to enact, and infused with checks and balances to protect minority interests. This stems in part from human nature: "Why fix what's not broken? It's worked so far."

Remember, also, that our survival instinct makes us strongly driven by *loss aversion*. Existing policies create constituencies, or special interests, which benefit from those policies. Policy changes that threaten to end or reduce those benefits are seen as losses by those special interests, so they are highly motivated to organize and fight against any proposed changes. Unfortunately, the beneficiaries of such reforms are not similarly motivated by unanticipated gains from better policies. We see this dynamic play out in almost every legislative fight; whether it concerns Social Security reform, corporate welfare reform, trade agreements, or union legislation. There is nothing more certain to get people out on the street, or concerned enough to contact their representative, than the possible loss of a treasured benefit.

The downside of this inherent bias toward the status quo is that necessary reforms that could avert crises are shelved until the crisis actually hits. Thus, nobody took a serious look at the rapidly transforming financial system until the whole system crashed. Nobody addressed the problems of government insured mortgages until Fannie Mae and Freddie Mac were forced into receivership. Nobody can fix government budgets because spending cuts and tax increases are largely rejected by voters. This even afflicts the private sector; General Motors continued to lose money until the U.S. taxpayer rescued it with a government bailout. Election politics leads to the demagoguery of fear over things like Social Security reform, yet continuing with the *status quo* threatens the surest disaster of all.

3.4 The Media

The media has traditionally been referred to as the <u>Fourth Estate</u>. As such, it is one of the pillars of a democratic society, keeping a watch over the three branches of government by providing information through a free press. This is the rationale behind the idea that freedom of the press is critical to a free society. A free press, however, is not always an unbiased press.

The American press has often been highly politicized in the past, so the fact that it is so again should not be surprising. Today, however, there are some very different conditions that affect the press, its editorial incentives, and our interaction with it.

The media can only survive as a business if it has a paying audience. A publisher or television station identifies a target audience and then attracts that audience by offering a product that is useful and entertaining. Thus, it is no surprise that urban newspapers appeal to their city's residents and rural newspapers likewise appeal to theirs. Subscriptions and advertising have been the primary revenue models for newspapers, magazines, and television media.

The development of alternative means of delivery, such as cable television and the Internet, has threatened the traditional media's existing revenue models and squeezed its profits. We now have more media chasing fewer profits and this inescapable financial reality has been influencing editorial content and policy. The pressure to survive has forced primary news media outlets to target their product more narrowly to an audience that is largely concentrated in metropolitan areas. The proliferation of alternative media, along with the declining cost structure of digital delivery, has led others to try and capture the non-metro audience with a differently tailored product. Thus we have talk radio, blogs, and the proliferation of cable news networks. In this competitive struggle to survive, news media have politicized themselves with partisan conflict in order to create controversy to attract readers and revenues. It is impossible to read a major urban newspaper and be unaware of its overt political bias. Editorial opinion soon becomes party propaganda. It's almost as if different media companies have become wholly owned subsidiaries of the two major political parties.

So, why have different media channels become so clearly defined by political ideology and partisanship? It seems inexplicable that, as the network broadcast industry was shrinking, a major new network was established (FOX) that quickly outpaced all of its long established rivals. Why do people watch either MSNBC or FOX? Why do they either read the New York Times, the Wall Street Journal, or listen to talk radio? The simple answer is: people seek opinions that reflect and confirm their own. But this still begs the question of why the news is so highly politicized.

3.5 Red vs. Blue?

I have investigated this puzzle over the past few election cycles. With the infamous 2000 presidential election, we first became aware of a red vs. blue geographic pattern in our national voting results. This pattern was most visibly stark in red-blue maps showing election returns based on county data. Most election data presented in the media are gathered from exit polling samples. However, exit polls focus on voter identity factors, such as sex, race, ethnicity, party affiliation, ideological identification, and former voting preferences. They do not account well for geographical differences and it is to geography that we must turn for an explanation of those red-blue maps. We officially tabulate election results according to counties and congressional districts. We also record census data by county. This allows us to compare all the actual voting data against the census profiles by county to see who is voting how. We have over 3000 different data points (3142 counties), an adequate sample to rule out various explanations, such as race, religion, or ethnicity. The data reveals some truths that contradicts the easy explanations offered by exit polls. *In reality, American voters' political preferences are correlated with the population densities of their communities and the lifestyles and ideologies associated with their communities.*

The media has offered many contradictory explanations, but it's difficult to argue with the data. We've been misinformed by a media and by party narratives that reach for simple sub-cultural identities as the causal factors of voting preferences. Supposedly, we've been told, we vote Republican or Democrat, conservative or liberal, based on religious preference, church attendance, gun ownership, country music or rap, pickup trucks or Priuses. This is all nonsense. These sub-cultural identities are merely associated with lifestyle preferences. The primary determinants of voting patterns are population density (whether one lives in an urban or rural/suburban community), marriage and household formation, and lastly, ideological preference (conservative and traditional vs. progressive and liberal). Roughly 40-50% of the voting patterns are explained by population density, 25-30% by marriage status, and 25-30% by ideological preference. All of these factors are positively correlated. Thus, married people who live in the country and who believe in traditional small town values tend to vote consistently to the ideological right of center. Singles who live in the city and advocate for change and reform tend to vote consistently to the ideological left of center. The important point is that *partisan preference is the least powerful predictor of these three factors.*

The geographic pattern has probably existed for the entire history of our democracy. Interestingly, the presidential electoral maps for 1896 look remarkably similar to the same maps for 2000 and 2004, albeit with the parties reversed. So, the only things that have really changed are the policies specifically chosen by the parties in order to gain votes and win elections. Remember, the rural South has always been conservative, but it has swung from being a solid Democratic stronghold to a solidly Republican one over the past half century. The parties changed, but the residents did not. Since the 1960s the Democrats have consistently courted young, urban populations while the Republicans have targeted older, rural populations. We can see how the areas of contention, i.e. the swing votes, are found in the suburban and exurban communities. As long as our two parties target these specific constituencies with narrow policies, we can expect these geographically-determined party preferences to persist, no matter who becomes president. We can also expect our media to accentuate these differences in order to appease their primary audiences.

I have briefly outlined above the three main factors shaping our political landscape: media, geographical differences, and party agendas. The geographical differences will remain, but the policy differences will always revolve around issues such as taxes vs. social spending, education funding, transportation and infrastructure spending, and individual liberty vs. communal priorities. The good news is that most differences on these issues are amenable to compromise. We can target taxes and spending and adjust each at the margins. We can reconcile education funding with the particular needs of the community while also maintaining quality standards. We can find solutions that meet communal priorities without sacrificing individual liberties. The issues that are not open to compromise are political positions that have hardened along biological identities, such as race, ethnicity, sex, and sexual orientation. Identity politics emphasizes our differences rather than our commonalities. How does one compromise one's biological or sexual identity? It cannot be done, and no one need have to.

I would argue that ideology is not really a problem for our politics. The majority of Americans are not ideologically rigid and I believe the ideologically charged labels of *conservative* and *liberal* have only led us down a cul-de-sac of inaccurate recriminations. I have written elsewhere that I believe the dominant ideology in American political culture is not best described as either conservative or liberal, but as what I would call *tolerant traditionalism*. On many issues, average Americans may be more conservative, but on many others we are open to change and tolerant of differences. The United States is one of the most religiously tolerant and religiously diverse societies in the world today. It is also one of the most racially tolerant and ethnically diverse. These characteristics make for a progressive and stable society. These are measures of our tolerant traditionalism.

It is doubtful that our media or political parties will change tactics without major pressures from their primary audiences. Political polarization works for these institutions. It helps them be successful. This will continue to be the case until viewers and voters force changes.

An interesting recent development in American politics is the rise of the Tea Party (TP). It's difficult to get an accurate handle on the Tea Party movement because it has become a political football that gets distorted by the media and by both parties. As a curious political analyst, I have observed Tea Party rallies and interviewed some of their participants. My sense is that this began as an amorphous movement of disaffected voters and ordinary citizens who were dissatisfied with recent trends in American politics. They spontaneously galvanized around the traditional American cultural values of individual liberty, self-reliance, and accountability. I fail to see the origins of the TP as rooted in partisanship, though political opportunists have clamored to associate themselves with this powerful political movement in order to claim its mission as their own. Conservatives have been most successful in this respect, as the small government principles espoused by the TP resonate more strongly with their ideological agenda. On the other side, we've seen liberal politicians decry the movement with attempts to promote themselves as the anti-Tea Party candidates. For certain politicians these tactics will be successful, but the voting public should not be fooled. The Tea Party is a voter rebellion generated by our dysfunctional politics. It is a grassroots, populist, anti-party movement. Where it goes from here is anyone's guess.

Since I first wrote this book, a new grassroots voter protest has arisen called OWS, for Occupy Wall Street. This movement seems less focused, but is primarily incensed over the dominance of financial and banking interests in our democracy. In that respect, I'm not sure they differ much from the Tea Party – both are protesting the political *status quo*.

3.6 Elites, Oligarchies, and Plutocracies

The last political issue that bears significantly on our political economy is the rise of powerful interest blocs that influence our political, financial, and media choices. I'm sure many readers will claim these have always controlled our politics. The Tea Party revolt may be a reaction to this (though I'm sure the Marxists among us will merely attribute its popularity to false consciousness).

The concentration of economic wealth has long been seen as a threat to democracy because of the power of money to control politics. I decline to describe this concentration as a conspiracy of rich and powerful elites. The rise of inequality in recent years has been less a deliberate action engineered by these elites than it is an inevitable byproduct of the communication, information, and financial revolutions. The capitalist revolution in the developing world has also brought the competition of roughly three billion more workers and middle class aspirants into the mix with globalization, helping to depress wage incomes.

The plunging costs of communication and information have transformed many of our production and distribution processes and yielded what has been called a *winner-take-all* society (WTA).[37] We no longer depend on and value local artists, craftspeople, products, professionals, celebrities, etc. Instead we have achieved immediate worldwide access to the proclaimed "best" of everything. The flip side of this accessibility and familiarity is that the proclaimed "best" in each and every industry or profession garners all the media attention and the wealth that is capitalized off their fame. One can hardly fault the celebrity chefs, talk show hosts, sports stars, movie stars, musicians, writers, politicians, CEOs, etc., but is this really how we want our culture to be shaped? And what can we do about it? I'm not sure. Nor am I sure it is necessary if we are careful to keep the WTA phenomenon in political perspective.

The political danger with a WTA society is that celebrity fame and economic mega-fortunes can translate into power to influence the democratic process, creating a plutocracy, a word of Greek origin meaning "rule by the wealthy." Thus, we see professional actors and celebrities advising us on politics and public policy and influencing election campaigns.[38] We can observe Wall Street banking elites dominating our policy institutions and we suffer professional politicians winning Oscars and Nobel Prizes for dubious achievements. Winner-take-all dynamics aggravate wealth and income inequalities and also feed back into political policies that reinforce the basic inequities.[39] Most recently we've seen how bankers have influenced the political class over financial regulation, then with the taxpayer-funded bailouts after the financial crash.

While we may not be able to blunt the economic power of fame or wealth, we can certainly change the policies that institutionalize the problem. A plutocracy should concern us gravely. The siphoning of wealth from savers, homeowners, and middle-class wage earners to wealthy bankers, creditors and an elite political class is the first step down the road to a plutocracy. The endpoint is a banana republic characterized by crony capitalism. I would suggest that the reversal of this trend towards crony capitalism lies less in attacking the machinations of the rich and powerful than in understanding how risk is shared, borne, and compensated in our political economy. With this knowledge we can transform our capitalism with the true powers of our free and democratic society: sheer magnitude of voters and consumers, networked coordination, market openness, transparency, and free competition.

CHAPTER FOUR

Applying the Model to Policy

4.1 The Great Moderation, The Credit Bubble and Financial Crises

In order to understand how we got where we are today, we need to familiarize ourselves with some recent economic history and U.S. policy responses. In the post-World War II period, the international monetary system was based on a fixed exchange rate regime established under the Bretton Woods Agreements of 1948. This regime established the U.S. dollar as the international reserve currency, anchored by a fixed exchange rate into gold. This meant that foreign banks could exchange their dollars for gold at the rate of $35 per ounce. This worked fine as long as there was a steady trade demand for dollars that was not outstripped by the supply. By the late 1960s, the excessive debt-driven spending of the Vietnam War and the Great Society social programs created an oversupply of dollars as the U.S. government spent in excess of tax receipts. Foreign banks, fearing the eventual depreciation of the dollar, demanded to exchange their dollar holdings for gold. [40] As U.S. gold reserves rapidly depleted, policymakers realized that the exchange system could not survive. In 1971, President Nixon abrogated the Bretton Woods Agreements, refusing to allow the U.S. Treasury to exchange dollars for gold at the $35 rate. In effect, he "closed the gold window," to preserve the gold reserves of the U.S.

Immediately, the price of gold rose to reflect this *de facto* depreciation of the dollar. As we discussed previously, the value of a currency is determined by what it can be exchanged for. If the sum of all the goods and services in the U.S. grows slower than the supply of the currency, the value of the currency will decline as each good or service will demand more of that currency to trade. This is inflation. In other words, prices of U.S. goods and services will rise in dollar terms (a haircut or restaurant meal will cost more), while dollar exchange rates against other currencies will fall (a trip to Paris will cost a lot more, while Europeans will flock to our shores to enjoy cheaper vacations in the States). By the early 1970s the dollar had become nominally overvalued and was then, by Nixon's policy change, losing value to bring prices back into equilibrium. It is important to understand that with the breakdown of Bretton Woods, the value of the U.S. dollar became untethered to anything of fixed real value, such as an ounce of gold. This meant that the dollar would become entirely subject to the policies that determine their supply and demand. Dollar supply is controlled by the private U.S. Federal Reserve system with Congressional oversight. We discussed this previously in the section, The Mystique of Money. Dollar demand is a function of real economic forces influenced by both monetary and fiscal policies.

The Nixon administration, in effect, transformed the international monetary system from a fixed exchange rate system, where currency values are fixed to each other, to a floating rate, fiat currency system where exchange markets determine the relative value of a currency on a daily basis based upon supply and demand. The U.S. dollar could no longer be converted into gold at $35 per ounce and could only be exchanged for whatever the markets determined its exchange value to be on any day.[41] The exchange value of the U.S. dollar began to "float" relative to all other currencies. This created the conditions for a market in competitive currencies—such as the British pound, the various European currencies (now replaced by the euro), the Japanese yen, the Swiss franc, and now the Chinese yuan—to trade against the dollar.

It is often said that controlling the supply of dollars to keep the U.S. economy on a steady growth path is like driving a car by using the rearview mirror. We never know when to step on the accelerator or the brake until it's too late. In other words, we don't know how many dollars is "right" until after we've veered off the road. (Not surprising, there have been a few crashes.) Why is the supply of dollars and their value important? Because the value or 'price' of the dollar affects every other price signal in the economy. In its role as the international reserve currency (central banks around the world hold dollar reserves and reconcile their trade payments accounts in dollars rather than in hundreds of various national currencies), the value of the U.S. dollar affects every other price signal *in the world*. If price signals are not accurate, there is little chance that our millions of individual economic decisions will be optimal.

What happened as a result of this new dollar policy? Because of the oversupply of dollars, inflationary forces buffeted the U.S. and world economy. This inflation was ineffectually, and temporarily, addressed by price and wage controls in the U.S. and international capital controls overseas. Then the world economy was hit by two unforeseen OPEC oil embargoes. While these embargoes were politically motivated to draw attention to the Arab-Israeli conflict, they were not unrelated to the declining value of the dollar. Oil is the major world commodity actually priced in U.S. dollars, so when oil exporters received less valuable dollars for their products, they had to raise their prices to compensate for the depreciation. Cutting the oil supply helped support the price increase.

By the end of the 1970s the U.S. economy had been in the doldrums for more than a decade. The so-called *misery index*, which added the inflation rate to the unemployment rate, reached a high of just over 20% as the election of 1980 approached. This led to a dramatic shift in monetary policy with President Carter's appointment of inflation hawk Paul Volcker as Chairman of the Federal Reserve. Under Carter and then Reagan, Volcker's mission was to break the back of inflationary expectations. He did this effectively in the early 1980s by shrinking the U.S. money supply, sending interest rates to 20% and spiking unemployment into double-digit levels. By 1984, inflation was broken and the U.S. economy bounced back as interest rates and unemployment receded.

Using the logic of our economic model, what was happening in the 1970s and 80s? How did the economy get out of equilibrium and what was required to get it back into balance? Before the breakdown of Bretton Woods, the world economy had gotten out of balance, as had the U.S. economy. U.S. government borrowing to spend on both the Vietnam War and Great Society welfare programs boosted consumption more than investment, while increasing the overall level of U.S. debt. Neither spending priority—military or welfare expenditures—did enough to increase the productive capacity of the U.S. economy. Thus, consumption demand outstripped production and, with accommodative monetary policy increasing the supply of dollars, prices rose.

How does inflation affect our simple model?[42] Inflation has the pernicious effect of creating uncertainty over future prices and future values. This raises nominal interest rates, which *should* cause people to consume less as they produce more. Inflation also erodes the value of savings and incomes, further causing people to save more and consume less. However, because prices are not stable and uncertain, the real interest rate (the nominal or actual interest rate minus the inflation rate) may actually be negative.[43] Negative real interest rates encourage borrowing and spending because the interest cost is negative, but the uncertain price environment will favor speculation in real assets, not investment in new production. So real estate prices rise, precious metal prices rise, art and other collectibles prices rise, but none of this hard asset speculation increases the productive capacity of the economy. What we end up with is the infamous "stagflation" of the late 1970s: slow growth, high unemployment, and rising prices. Inflation distorts economic incentives and impedes the reallocation of resources that would get a stalled economy back onto a stable growth path. Volcker's policy to reduce the money supply with high real interest rates sharply corrected this inflationary price distortion, but at considerable cost in unemployment and productive capacity underutilization. In other words, Volcker and the central bank engineered a steep recession.

Once inflationary expectations were eliminated and prices stabilized, interest rates gradually declined as they lost the uncertainty premium tacked onto lending rates to compensate for inflation. Asset bubbles in gold and silver burst and investment was channeled back into productive activities. Reagan enacted tax reductions as part of his supply-side economic policy, arguing that lower taxes on productive activity would increase the returns to investment. The twin effect of eliminating inflation and lowering taxes on production meant that risks were reduced while returns increased, so the risk-adjusted rate of return to investment got a double boost. The results were highly favorable, but were perhaps less due to the immutable logic of supply-side economic policy and more to the fact that the misguided policies of the 1970s had severely depressed productive capacity. My point is that the debates between the competing theories of Keynesian demand and supply-side economic policies often ignore the context of whether the problem is inadequate demand, disincentives to production, or both.[44]

The limits to the success of the Volcker-Reagan supply-side corrective became apparent by the end of the 1980s as the economy slowed. The economy's saving grace was probably the technological innovation wave in microchips, computers, and networked communications during the 1990s. The new Federal Reserve Chairman Alan Greenspan was dubbed "The Maestro" for his benign monetary policy that helped finance this technological and economic revolution. The only hiccups were a series of international financial crises that engulfed Mexico, Thailand, Korea, Argentina, and Russia (not mere hiccups to those living in these countries). These crises were mostly due to the massive financial flows on international capital markets that accompanied the explosion of exchange rate trading in the new floating rate monetary regime after 1971. Developing countries that liberalized their economies could attract massive inflows of capital that could and did reverse when financial circumstances changed. This capital was often loaned and invested in a developing country's growing economy, but then the capital that financed these investments could be withdrawn at a moment's notice, forcing the country to the brink of bankruptcy. Often the loans were priced in U.S. dollars, while the country's local investment returns were received in local currencies. A financial crisis meant a crash in the domestic currency and almost certain bankruptcy with the inability to pay off the loans in U.S. dollars. This was the case in Russia, which defaulted on its debts in 1998. But the Federal Reserve rescued the world financial system from the Russian crisis with liquidity (i.e. lots of cheap credit in the U.S. to shore up U.S. credit markets), while the International Monetary Fund (mostly funded by U.S. taxpayer funds) came to the rescue with conditional bailouts for the beleaguered countries. This all seemed to work at the time and the U.S.

economy, together with the world economy, marched on. Unfortunately, all the dollar liquidity sloshing around in the economy meant we were just heading off another precipice.

The excess liquidity in the U.S. economy became apparent with the Internet bubble of 2000. The mania of this period saw stock fortunes made and lost in matters of days and weeks, with new companies selling for incomprehensible values just because they had a .com in their names. This is the nature of financial euphoria—it causes investors to chase ever higher prices of financial assets until these collapse like a party balloon meeting a pin. We will experience these types of bubbles and busts again and again. But it is important to note that all financial asset bubbles *must* be financed with credit. This is where the Federal Reserve went seriously wrong in the first decade of the 21st century.

When the Internet bubble burst, the real economy was not seriously affected because most of the money lost was "funny money" anyway. Unemployment was barely effected and the recession of 2001-2 that followed was notable for the 2000 presidential election that was decided by the Supreme Court, a slew of corporate scandals that often accompany financial manias, and the terrorist attacks of 9/11 that occurred before the economy had found its footing. There is a good case to be made that the recession was aggravated by poor Federal Reserve policy, which first raised interest rates too high in late 2000 and then pushed them too low for too long after the economy stalled in 2002. Recall from our model that manipulating the interest rate distorts the signals that govern our decisions to consume or save, borrow, or invest. In late 2002, the economic policymakers were faced with a moribund stock market, businesses that were retrenching and neither borrowing nor investing, banks had no corporate borrowers, and investors who were jaded by corporate scandals and the deflated tech bubble. Nevertheless, Federal Reserve policy found a new belle to take to the ball: the housing market.

4.1.1 A House is Not Just a Home?

Starting in 2002, the Federal Reserve helped push interest rates down to 1% and held them there for almost three years to encourage credit creation. I say 'helped' because there was also a world savings glut caused by the high savings rates in rapidly growing economies, such as India's and China's, which also put downward pressure on interest rates. These excess Asian savings found their way to U.S. and European consumers mostly by refinancing and expanding the world housing stock. A lower interest rate allows a buyer to purchase more house with the same income, or refinance at a lower rate and withdraw equity from his or her existing home. U.S. policymakers such as Greenspan, who believed that the world had attained a new, stable plateau of low inflation, balanced GDP growth, and reduced risk, welcomed this new 'stimulus' strategy. These new conditions engendered a rising confidence in the future that justified permanently low interest rates and higher valuations of capital. Greenspan argued that additional consumption demand from refinancing and home equity withdrawals would keep the economy humming along until the corporate sector started expanding. If only we had reached such a Nirvana.

To understand what was happening we need to examine the process in greater detail. First, when banks create credit through lending, they control the risks of nonpayment by several methods. If you've ever applied for a bank loan, you are familiar with these. Most obvious is the past credit history of the borrower, but most important for the lender is securing loan <u>collateral</u> that can be claimed in case of default. This, ironically, is why banks are happy to lend money to people who don't need it. Collateral value can be represented by liquid financial assets, like savings or Treasury bonds in the bank, or real assets, such as a house. When we secure a home mortgage from a lender, the lender holds a lien on our house. If the bank fails to receive mortgage payments, it can exercise this lien by foreclosing on the mortgage and repossessing the house. Then it sells the house to recapture its loan investment.

All loans created by the banking and the shadow banking systems were backed by some form of collateral. In the residential mortgage market, the collateral was represented by rising home values. In the shadow banking system, collateral was represented by complex financial derivatives, mostly collateralized loans based on these same home values. In the last twenty years, banks' careful monitoring of the collateral value of their loans has been weakened by a financial innovation known as <u>securitization</u>. Securitization is an effective risk management technique whereby many different loans with different characteristics can be pooled together to reduce credit risk through diversification. This asset pool of loans can be packaged into a new financial security for resale to investors. In this manner, the payments on the loan go to the new investor/owners together with the credit risk of default. If the home owner defaults, the issuing bank is out of the picture and the investors lose. The bank no longer bears that risk of default so it has less incentive to care about the quality of the loans it originates. Through securitization, banks were able to ramp up credit creation with little concern for the risks of borrower creditworthiness or the value of the collateral. (This is the first hint that all is not going to end well with this story.) For financial markets in general, securitized pools of mortgages and other <u>collateralized debt obligations</u> created a vast new market for tradable credit instruments.

As with all financial bubbles, there was a positive feedback process at work between house prices, mortgages, and credit creation. The subsidized low interest rates promoted by the Fed, combined with the world glut in savings, distorted incentives for both borrowers and lenders. Exotic mortgage products and cheap credit encouraged people to buy houses or refinance existing homes. The loans were then pooled and repackaged to be sold off to investors around the world. The proceeds of these sales were then channeled back into new credit creation with more loans. Easy credit meant more unmet demand for new homes, driving home prices higher. Higher home prices increased the value of the underlying collateral for the entire mortgage derivatives market, generating new credit for more loans. The positive feedback between new credit creation driving home prices higher, along with their collateral loan values, promoted more credit creation to satisfy housing demand. The end result was a bubble in the values of all collateralized financial assets. Home owners, for instance, were borrowing based on home values that were unrealistically priced. The financial derivatives were also overpriced according to these overvalued homes. The bubble fever soon spread to the shopping malls and auto dealers as homeowners borrowed against home equity to buy, buy, buy.

The banks' frantic search for new borrowers to keep this business going eventually led down a slippery slope until the only prospects left were borrowers who really couldn't afford a loan for an overpriced house or car. These were the subprime borrowers who applied for the infamous 'liar' and 'NINJA' loans: no job, no income, and no assets. All that was required by the lenders was the ability to fog a mirror and the "American Dream" of owning a home. That dream also became a clarion call for politicians seeking voter support by encouraging subsidized mortgage lending through the government home mortgage agencies known as Fannie Mae and Freddie Mac.[45]

Unfortunately, while all this debt-driven buying was going on, nobody was watching the store. The risks of mortgage loans were sold off to unsuspecting investors in the form of securitized debt instruments. These poor innocents put their trust in these securities because they were rated AAA by credit agencies such as Moody's, Fitch, and Standard and Poor's. As quasi-government agencies with strong political support, Fannie and Freddie were seen as guaranteed by the Federal government. Nobody had incentives to monitor the risks at the source of all this financial alchemy: the inherent creditworthiness of the borrowers or the intrinsic value of the underlying collateral.

If we refer back to our model, we can see exactly what was happening. Economic growth was being funded by massive amounts of subsidized credit and debt. The recapitalization of the housing market did not create newfound wealth; it merely raised the valuation of existing assets.[46] In other words, we mostly lived in the same houses that we always did, they were now just worth much more in nominal dollar terms. Enough to finance a new Mercedes and a luxury cruise. Money for nothing? This is a neat trick if you can pull it off.

Alas, what goes up must come down. Or in the case of interest rates, what goes down must come back up. When interest rates finally did begin to rise in 2005 and 2006, home prices started to weaken and the positive feedback cycle quickly reversed. Regrettably, this is what happens with credit and debt cycles, and the down cycles can be far more brutal. Subprime home owners began to default, causing securitized mortgage investments to plunge in value. This depressed the collateral values that backed up home loans and the derivatives of those loans. Soon the interdependent derivatives markets created by the vast expansion of securitized debt began to crash like cascading dominoes. All collateral values went into a free-fall, creating confusion and uncertainty throughout the financial industry over the values of all its complex credit instruments. The meltdown caused a credit crunch in corporate overnight lending, as all trust in valuations was shattered and nobody was willing to extend any credit. This is what occurred in late summer of 2007. But the debt spiral continued to feed on itself.

In a credit downturn, loan assets, like houses and stocks, must be sold to cover debts and loan recalls, depressing the prices of these assets further. This sets off a chain reaction of more defaults throughout the economy as prices, investment, and production contract. A collapse in the general price level is what we call deflation. Deflation is the opposite of inflation. In periods of deflation, prices drop. This sounds delightful for consumers, but it creates a serious problem when expectations of falling prices cause buyers to delay purchases to wait for prices to drop further. This causes businesses to fail if they either do not sell their goods and services or do so at a loss. Unemployment rises as workers are laid off, driving consumption demand even lower.

Deflation in a debt-driven economy is even more catastrophic. As economic activity declines, debts must still be paid in full or go into default. Most homeowners understand this. If both their incomes and house values fall, they still have to repay the full amount of their mortgage loan. As people default on their debts, available credit shrinks as banks rebuild their capital reserves instead of making new loans. The money supply is effectively contracting, causing the purchasing power of the currency to rise. If goods are cheaper, each dollar buys more goods. Debts previously incurred, however, must now be paid with dearer dollars. At the same time, incomes and wages that service these debts are shrinking, causing more defaults. Forced asset sales to pay debts drive prices ever lower. We've seen this in the housing meltdown. Incomes and house values have fallen, but mortgage debts remain the same, meaning more homeowners slip into insolvency and banks foreclose on their homes, driving house prices even lower. This further depresses economic activity, which pushes more homeowners to the brink.

A deflationary spiral is a vicious downward cycle. The psychological effect is a complete loss of confidence, with a desire to hoard real assets as protection against an uncertain, frightening future. Productive activity comes to a halt. This is akin to the economy being slowly dragged off a cliff as businesses and banks are forced into insolvency. This is somewhat what happened in the 1930s with the Great Depression. It was not a pretty picture.

The financial crisis that began to roil the markets in 2007 came to a head in fall of 2008 when the credit markets froze. The financial market meltdown and contagion risked a full-blown deflationary spiral and a potential world-wide depression. All the central banks and world governments were forced to step in and provide trillions of dollars/euros/yuan/yen in support of an imploding financial system.

Imagine the economy is a hot air balloon that is constantly rising as we overheat the credit burners. When leaks develop and the hot air of financial euphoria finally begins to cool, the credit begins to contract. As the cooler air compresses, or leaks out, the balloon begins to collapse at an alarming rate. This was the state of the world economy when governments began to pump more hot air (i.e. bailouts and credit, now funded by taxpayers), into the balloon to keep it from crashing to earth. The result of these government actions is the replacement of shrinking private credits with public credits backed by an unprecedented expansion of public debt. The goal was to save the banks and the financial system from a catastrophic meltdown that would threaten the non-financial world economy. However, public debt is a liability that must be paid off from future government revenues, so the servicing of this debt must be paid from increased direct or indirect taxes on the population.[47] In effect, we now find ourselves having traded a private debt bubble for a public one.

We are not yet out of the woods, by any estimate. If government tax receipts cannot cover the increase in debt service, the government, through the U.S. Treasury, will have to issue more public debt. Debt service by borrowing always explodes exponentially as one must continually borrow to service rising debt levels. It is the ultimate Ponzi scheme, with only one possible outcome: a massive, deflationary crash.[48] Without sound corrective policies, this is the place we may all soon find ourselves.

The housing boom and bust was a typical case of financial euphoria, similar to many in history, such as the 17th century's tulip bulb mania in Holland and the South Sea Bubble in 1720. It was surprising because it came so closely on the heels of the dot-com bubble. The trillion dollar question that nobody asked the policymakers was: If all housing prices were booming around the world because of low interest rates, what would happen when interest rates began to rise? What would happen when the value of collateral fell? We know from our model that interest rates rise and fall in order to keep the economy on a stable path. Interest rates are the principal 'governor' that regulates economic decisions over time. If rates stay permanently low, investment in the future will dry up as present consumption dominates. (This is just another way of saying there's no tomorrow, or "the world is ending!") How did we miss this fundamental truth?

Over the past two-plus decades we have experienced economic growth funded by an expanding credit and debt bubble. Our simple economic model shows that credit borrowing that is invested in order to increase future production can add to our stock of wealth. If the investment is productive, future consumption will not have to be reduced in order for the debt to be paid off. But credit that is used to increase present consumption rather than present investment will require a reduction in future consumption in order to repay the debt. From 2002 to 2008, we did not defer our consumption to save and invest. Instead, we borrowed heavily so that we could keep consuming and speculating on assets. Had we chosen instead to invest our borrowing in profitable investments, our GDP and incomes would have grown and we wouldn't be in this mess. But a housing asset bubble is not profitable for society; it is mostly illusory wealth.

It should be apparent that the policies of the past 30-40 years will be inappropriate policies for the future. It is also unlikely that the economic choices we have all made over this period will be the same going forward. Over the next decade or two we will discover just how wisely or unwisely we have spent our bailout and stimulus money. As many pundits have said, *we cannot borrow and spend our way to prosperity*. With an aging population, we also face some major demographic changes that will have a profound impact on all our policy choices and decisions.

From a policy perspective, this is the crux of the matter. As our economy slowly recovers, we will discover how much damage has been inflicted on our economic well-being. Savings rates have already increased significantly. But increased saving behavior is fighting against policies that are trying to induce more borrowing and spending.

And lest we forget, all this credit is *fiat* money, backed by the full faith and credit of governments that seem wholly incapable of applying prudent economic policies in the long-term interests of their citizens. This frightening reality now circles the globe, from Japan to China to India to Europe to the U.S.A.

4.2 The Policy Agenda

At this point one might be tempted to ask, incredulously, what were the so-called policy experts thinking?! As we discussed earlier, our leaders focus primarily on economic growth and employment as solutions to every problem. So they seek every way to stoke the engine of GDP growth with the tools they have—loose credit promoted by Federal Reserve policy, government spending authorized by Congress, and tax cuts. But, to reiterate, *we cannot borrow and spend our way to prosperity*. Instead, we must invest our scarce resources efficiently and profitably. One does not need an economics degree to understand this (apparently, having one doesn't necessarily mean one understands it either). As policy critics, we can be generous and concede that to err is human. We do, however, need a way to correct our errors before they become catastrophic. And we need to learn from our mistakes. Though the rescue of the financial system from the crisis of 2008 was necessary, the danger is that we may not have learned the prudent policy lessons from this disaster.

Let us step back and use our model to think about how the economy departs from, and then returns, to equilibrium. We humans make mistakes: we open restaurants that fail in short order; we open boutiques for pets that fizzle; our investment ideas are not always brilliant. But what happens if the financiers of our bad ideas keep giving us more credit? A deep hole becomes a chasm that can swallow us whole. It is the same case with loose credit subsidized by the entire banking system. The situation only worsens when bad ideas that fail get bailed out just so they can fail again, but even bigger, another day. This is merely postponing the day of reckoning.

The super credit cycle that we experienced from 1982 to 2008 has distorted many prices and induced many inefficiencies across the economy. A price crash, or a recession, is the market's way of realigning prices to where goods once again become attractive for an exchange between buyers and sellers. When our economic policies cause, or allow, the economy to outrace itself at a rate that is unsustainable, eventually the prices of financial assets, as well as real assets, collapse as the economy contracts. After a bubble, stock prices, housing prices, energy prices, and retail goods prices all collapse. As wage rates fall, labor must be reallocated to more productive uses, which entails unemployment. When the dust settles, we pick ourselves up off the floor and rebuild.

Of course, a good policy agenda would insure that price distortions never percolate into a bubble. Once the pot has begun to boil, however, the quickest remedy is a price reset.[49] The architects of our recent economic policies have done their best to resist an asset price reset, in the hopes that we can draw out the adjustment process over time without a complete financial market failure. This strategy is prudent policy management given that the financial system was broken, but the sooner we get back to prices that reflect economic fundamentals, the sooner the economy can get back to a balanced growth equilibrium.

We know that the valuation of capital is heavily dependent on some ephemeral feeling of confidence; when pessimism reigns, capital can be devalued in an instant. Our policymakers surely want to avoid price declines that overshoot fundamental values because of pessimism or perceptions of unchecked price deflation. This is politically understandable but doesn't make the current policies ideal. We can see their results—stock and commodities prices boom ahead, while unemployment stays unchanged or increases. This cannot last; capital must be redeployed into productive uses, or the price collapse will be even steeper next time. The policymakers are fighting Mr.

Market but, in the end, Mr. Market always wins.[50]

At this point we should turn the discussion away from past mistakes toward a more winning formula for the future. For a comprehensive and consistent policy approach, we should first articulate a guiding philosophy that will help orient our analysis. Without this guiding philosophy we may only discover after the fact that many policies are contradictory and counterproductive. I will take our constitutional principles as a starting point. With these in hand, I will offer appropriate guiding principles given what we know about the economy and the policy tools we have at our disposal. There is much room for debate and disagreement over the political and social goals of policy and what trade-offs are acceptable or preferred. We will not get bogged down in those subjective differences, but, suffice to say, this is where the political divide fractures and the heated debate begins.

A conventional approach to formulating policy is to identify a problem, consider several solutions with rudimentary cost-benefit analyses, choose the best solution that is politically viable, and then move on to the next problem. It should be apparent to anyone paying attention that this method is wholly inadequate. First, cost-benefit analysis assumes we can predict how behavior will change, or not change, after the policy is enacted. Our behavioral models in the social sciences are inadequate to this task, the upshot being that we cannot assess the necessary trade-offs in choosing one policy over another.[51]

Second, existing policy programs are rarely revisited and re-evaluated. If the policy solution was successful, and the problem solved, shouldn't the program end? And if the program was unsuccessful, shouldn't we scrap it and start over? What actually happens is that the new problems created by applying the wrong policies demand more policy solutions, and so we layer bad policies upon bad policies and wonder why the problem is never solved. (This is somewhat how we distorted the healthcare market beyond all rational recognition, and now propose to fix it with a bureaucratically controlled, Rube Goldberg solution.)

Third, one of the most serious mistakes we make in designing and evaluating economic and social policies is to focus on the observable consequences and not the hidden ones. This is referred to as the law of unintended consequences, best illustrated by the broken window fallacy.[52] If a child breaks a window, we might think that this creates work for the glazier, whose wife then spends the money at the market and so on, stimulating demand across the economy. But this ignores the fact that the owner of the window will now not spend that money he had to pay the glazier for something else, like a new suit, thereby hurting the tailor, etc. Now, this common-sense analogy does not apply so well to government spending under a fiat currency, since the monetary authorities can create new deficit spending out of thin air and not crowd out private sector spending. However, that doesn't mean there are not unintended consequences.

Public goods markets do not create accurate price signals since the government creates the supply by mandate and often subsidizes the price and thus the demand. There are no price signals that indicate whether the public goods provision is optimal or efficient. For instance, we never know if the U.S. Postal Service is efficient or not and what the true price of delivering a letter is. This suggests that the public sector will be less efficient than private markets but through government subsidies will be able to out-compete private companies and drive them out of business, thereby creating a government monopoly. If we are merely substituting public spending for private spending, we may be gaining less and paying more.[53] This is an important point to consider when we increase public spending and confirms our intuition that we cannot borrow and spend our way to prosperity. Economic policies must always consider what Sherlock Holmes referred to as "the dog that didn't bark."

To begin, our guiding philosophy should reinforce our immutable constitutional principles of freedom and democratic justice. These principles establish that the rights of life, liberty, and the pursuit of happiness are lodged within the individual. It is important to remember this. Economics, politics, and social policy serve a greater good beyond economic and physical security. Cuba claims to provide equality and economic security to all its citizens through income support and free health care, for instance. But it does so at the greater cost of a loss of liberty and basic freedoms that we in the U.S. take for granted. So, our first principle for policy is:

1. **Economic policy and politics should serve the principles of freedom; in the realm of public policy this translates into maximizing** *freedom of choice* **and** *freedom of action*.[54]

We have discussed how the economy sustains itself over time by constantly reallocating resources between consuming, saving, investing, and borrowing. Our second principle for policy flows from this understanding:

2. **Policies should facilitate the flexibility of the economy, its adaptability to unpredictable change, and the fluid reallocation of resources. This requires accurate price signals provided by competitive, functioning markets.**[55]

Among the programs we have instituted in the past, a policy anomaly exists that reveals something important about our priorities. While the proposals of politicians and policy experts try to expand economic growth at all costs, the programs that have actually been delivered are designed to manage risk with social insurance and welfare transfers. This leads me to conclude that our political demands reflect *the dominance of loss aversion in our policy preferences.* Social Security (a retirement income program), Medicare (a retirement healthcare program), Medicaid (a healthcare safety net), and assorted insurance-based compensation programs for unemployment and disability consume the bulk of our government expenditures. Direct spending on these programs constitutes roughly 57% of the Federal budget. When we include military spending, which defends us from risks to our national security, plus interest on the debt, the share comes to roughly 80%. Most of the remaining 20% is spent on the bureaucratic administration of these various programs. This spending pattern is mirrored in the fifty state budgets.

This would appear to confirm what evolutionary and behavioral psychology tells us: What citizens really want is life, liberty, and the pursuit of happiness *subject to* an acceptable level of risk that ensures our survival and well-being. When we feel we cannot manage these risks ourselves, we have overwhelmingly voted to have them managed through public programs. What we have really created with our democracy is not a free market, capitalist society supporting a small welfare state, but a social insurance state in its entirety.[56]

Politicians and policymakers single-mindedly pursuing economic growth do not have things wrong. The accumulation of wealth through economic growth is one of the best self-insurance policies, and the ultimate source, through taxes and redistribution, of any social provision. But with respect to policies, the goal of maximizing material welfare through economic growth is not the same as insuring society against loss. Economic growth requires increasing risk-taking investment; insuring against loss demands better collective and individual risk management. These two policy goals should complement each other, as better risk management empowers greater risk-taking. Our quest for economic growth can serve our desire to be secure, but it should *not* violate the more important desire of freedom of choice. Our survival instinct demands that we manage our private risks prudently (an amusing reference to the Darwin Awards comes to mind), but the logic of democratic politics will often lead to perverse results with the public management of risk. Systemic risk in our financial sector and impending budgetary crises in Social Security and Medicare are two cases in point. To save these programs, we need to change them.

Let us also consider the context of the world in which we live. It is uncertain and constantly changing. Our economic and political policies and institutions must enable us to adapt and manage this change in whatever form it comes. Rigidity and inflexibility is a recipe for disaster, as the experience of any fossilized dinosaur might attest. To restate Charles Darwin's quote cited at the beginning of this book: "It is not the strongest of the species that survive, nor the most intelligent, *but the one most responsive to change*." Universal social insurance policies are, necessarily, of a one-size-fits-all variety. They sacrifice individual freedom of choice and preference in favor of centralized efficiency, an efficiency that usually never materializes. We chose these programs in the past, but as technology and social organization evolve, new possibilities for managing these risks have arisen. How many people had 401(k)s in 1945? Or invested in foreign currency funds? The point is that our risk-management tools have evolved—our political and social institutions must evolve as well.

We should only resort to social insurance if there is no better option. Instead, our economic markets should to be fluid and responsive in their allocation of resources over time and our public policies should reinforce nature's imperative to adapt to change. This yields the next policy principle:

3. **To facilitate the management of change, public policies should primarily focus on managing risk; first by helping citizens manage their own risks; second by insuring functioning private insurance markets; and lastly, by providing social insurance.**

4.2.1 Private and Social Insurance

As we discussed in Chapter Two, in a closed system there is really only one way to manage the risk and uncertainty associated with change: diversification. While nature diversifies with biological species that randomly adapt over long periods of time, we must diversify financially by accumulating capital and distributing it across broad classes of financial assets. This is the logic underlying any and every insurance and retirement plan. For example, pension funds or 401(k)s accumulate payroll savings that are pooled and reinvested into diversified portfolios of financial and real assets. The same applies to our accident, homeowners, or automobile insurance, except these only pay out if we suffer a loss.

On the public side, Social Security is a diversified income security insurance pool that collects contributions from almost all working members of society and is paid out to current retirees according to set formulas.[57] Social Security insurance is different than a pure insurance model in that the funds are not saved and reinvested over time to achieve additional returns. Transferring funds from young to old makes Social Security highly dependent on demographics and the overall growth potential of the economy.

All insurance pools, public and private, suffer from moral hazard and adverse selection. Adverse selection occurs when low-risk participants opt out of a pool because they feel the premium cost is too high given their individual risk profile. As these low-risk participants opt out, premiums must rise to reflect the higher risk profile of the remaining pool, causing even more low-risks to opt out. In the end, only high-risk participants will remain in the pool with prohibitive premiums. The concentration of bad risks defeats the goal of diversification. An example is when good drivers opt out of auto insurance pools, leaving only an undiversified pool of bad drivers who raise the cost of insurance. The problem posed by adverse selection is often solved by compulsory participation or mandates, but there is still a self-sorting problem of low-cost, low-risk vs. high-cost, high-risk pools. This problem afflicts our health insurance industry for patients with pre-existing conditions.

We defined moral hazard briefly in Chapter Two, but let us reexamine the concept here. Moral hazard describes a situation of information asymmetry where the insured changes his/her behavior because they have insurance, but the insurer is unaware. An example of moral hazard is a person who drives more recklessly because he/she's insured. This increases the possibility of unexpected losses to the insurer. The only way to reduce moral hazard is to monitor the insured's behavior, which is why auto insurers raise or lower premiums based on one's driving records and accidents. Implicit in the notion of moral hazard is the idea that incentives between the two parties are misaligned. If their incentives were perfectly aligned, the information asymmetry and the monitoring would be superfluous. (Self-insurance through personal savings is a case where incentives are perfectly aligned, thus, there is no moral hazard.)

Like private insurance pools, social insurance programs like Social Security and Medicare also suffer the costs of moral hazard (because of adverse selection, participation is compulsory for most citizens). For example, people expecting Social Security often reduce their private savings for retirement. Since the government also is not 'saving' Social Security payroll taxes, there is a net loss of savings to the economy. A smaller supply of savings means interest rates must rise, reducing investment returns in economic production and growth. This reduces national wealth and tax revenues, which Social Security depends upon to meet its obligations. Indirectly, we see the magnitude of this moral hazard cost in the unfunded liabilities of the Social Security system, now at a level of $15 trillion.[58]

The problem is more egregious with Medicare, as the provision of free healthcare in old age encourages people to indulge unhealthy habits and overuse healthcare services, which increases the total costs of care. The main problem with social insurance is that there is no agent, or agency, able to monitor the behavior of pool participants, as is done with private insurance pooling. We each pay the same level of taxes, whether we are good risks or bad risks. Good risks are thus penalized for good behavior and bad risks are subsidized for bad behavior. What can we expect except an increase in bad risk behavior and exploding costs?

With self-insurance there are no moral hazard or adverse selection costs—the inherent informational costs associated with insurance pools and their misaligned incentives are eliminated when we internalize them to the individual. Most people do self-insure to a certain extent against the contingencies of old-age or health. We call it saving. This propensity to manage unforeseen contingent risk is summed up in the iconic phrase: "Save for a rainy day." It seems unlikely that public policies encouraging us to do otherwise (i.e., no need to save, the government will take care of you) will give us the results (security) we desire. The more important non-economic benefit of self-insurance is that it empowers individual freedom and choice. We own our savings, we can invest them as we see fit, and upon our death, we can leave the remainder to anyone we choose. We enjoy none of these freedoms with social insurance.

The main point of this section is to demonstrate how private insurance is superior to social insurance in almost every way. Why, then, do we even have social insurance? The reason is because of the incompleteness or failures of private insurance markets. There is no easy way to insure against the loss of a job, so we have socialized unemployment insurance. Insurance pooling is also inadequate if loss events are not independent or if their probability of occurring approaches unity, or one. Think of a company insuring against a natural disaster, such as an earthquake, hurricane, or flood. All the insured parties within the path of this disaster suffer losses together. The losses are related, or dependent. The insurance pool that includes all these parties is unable to cover the losses and the insurer goes bankrupt.[59] Because insurance is difficult to obtain for these losses, federal programs, such as FEMA, are often the only way to receive compensation. A person with a pre-existing health condition is a case where the probability of that loss event occurring is one—a sure thing. A universal catastrophic social insurance plan based on the incidence or probability of such illnesses or diseases is one proffered solution to the case of pre-existing conditions. We should not disavow the need for social insurance, as democratic justice demands that we protect citizens from the vagaries of chance. It is most efficient, however, when it is used as a complement, not as a substitute, for private insurance markets.

Some advocates justify social insurance by arguing that it can contribute to a sense of communal interdependence and solidarity in the face of risk or disaster. With universal social insurance, all citizens receive the same protection and share the same fate, so there is little conflict between winners and losers. There is considerable value to political solidarity within a democratic polity, but this can be achieved without the onerous financial cost incurred by runaway liabilities associated with moral hazard. We should consider private-public solutions to risk management that involve narrower, loss-based, catastrophic social insurance pools in conjunction with wider, private, self-insurance methods. Think of how we combine 401(k)s and IRAs with Social Security. The more successful private self-insurance is, the less dependent we are on social insurance and uncontrolled public liabilities. It is an error to believe that social insurance provides the only viable solution to our risk management needs. The bottom line is that we need policies that encourage us all to produce and save throughout our lives for contingent risks. The following corollaries should be added to policy principle #3 on risk management:

i. The preferred policy for risk management is self-insurance

through increased savings and diversified asset holdings;

ii. **The next policy priority should be to insure functioning and competitive private insurance markets;**

iii. **In cases of insurance market incompleteness or failure, policy should resort to universal social insurance systems funded by taxed contributions; ideally these contributions can be based on the actuarial experience of losses so that the insurance system is financially sound. Social insurance essentially provides a minimum safety net.**

4.2.2 Distributional Issues

One of the most persistent criticisms against market economies is the problem of economic inequality, in terms of both income and wealth. I will define this as a distributional issue that is rooted in risk-bearing and in the political or economic power that determines who bears the risk and who controls the returns. Proponents of market outcomes often cite evidence of the mobility of incomes and wealth, in that poor people often become richer in absolute terms and inequality is just a temporary artifact of a fluid society. The more important issue for them is national wealth and the belief that a rising tide lifts all boats. But this argument is unconvincing by itself.

First, relative wealth matters in a world of scarce resources. Think of the successful Stanford professor who earns a good salary, but must compete with Silicon Valley neighbors to buy a house. It is of little benefit to know he could live rather well in Oklahoma on the same salary.

Second, wealth can confer political power that can influence the formulation of policies that reinforce that wealth and power. This exposes democratic society to the risk of plutocracy, whereby the winners of a winner-take-all society get to make the rules under which that society operates. This can only lead to a banana republic in which the wealthy political class makes all the laws and reinterprets the constitution to favor their particular interests.

Third, when markets function well and economic growth is positive, the returns to capital concentrate to the successful, at least initially. The more successful a business is in maximizing its profits (often by reducing labor costs), the more residual profit of production is returned to the owners of the business. In other words, those who successfully bear the risks get richer and those who do not either receive the same, or less, compensation. We can observe this in the immediate results of outsourcing production to cheap labor countries. Labor costs drop, leading to higher profits for existing owners. (My point is not to condemn outsourcing or the rationalization of production, as these both can add to national wealth, but only to recognize the real distributional effects.) Successful adjustment can occur only if the domestic resources that have been idled (such as skilled workers) are redeployed to more profitable uses. That's a big "if," as any middle manager now knows, and in the meantime the distributional costs are borne unevenly by those who are displaced.

Fourth, I will make a controversial claim that inequality imposes economic, as much as political and social, costs upon a democratic capitalist society by depressing economic growth. Think back to our earlier discussion of trade and exchange: The basis of exchange depends upon the ability of both parties to offer something of value to one another. If one party holds all the wealth, there is no basis of exchange beyond subsistence labor, as existed with feudalism. What happens in our simple model if the rich keep getting richer and the poor get poorer? Total aggregate demand must decline and excess investment capital, in the hands of the rich, will chase decreasing returns as the value of idle capital dissipates. This causes investment capital to fuel asset price bubbles, first in the stock and commodity markets and then in real asset classes like precious metals, collectibles and real estate.[60] Imagine also that government policymakers, seeing the decline in demand, step in to stimulate consumption with deficit spending and loose credit? This merely fans the flames of resource misallocation with more asset booms that lead to busts. This should all sound familiar.

4.2.3 Capitalism For All

Whether one accepts the propositions in the previous paragraph or not, there is a set of solutions that can address the problems of inequality and also serve the objectives of good economic policy. The main idea behind this set of solutions is the promotion of widespread capital accumulation across the population and its subsequent reinvestment in diversified asset portfolios. Individual portfolios of capital assets would not only grow in value as the economy grew, they would be available to mitigate the risks we face in an uncertain world. In other words, we would solve our needs for security in the only tried and true method possible: through savings for self-insurance and through diversification of wealth. This yields the following policy principle:

4. **Capital is the lifeblood of a free market society. Economic policies should promote capital accumulation and widespread participation in capital ownership.**[61]

The 'democratization' of capital can open up capital markets through microfinance, giving wider access to competitive sources of investment capital. This is historically how poor immigrant communities have bootstrapped their way to wealth. Since participation in the wealth-creating potential of a market economy would be more widely shared by all, an increase in capital investment combined with available labor can drive that potential higher.

We cannot ignore the fact that widespread accumulation of capital also demands widespread risk-sharing, which is the basis for spreading returns. One might think more risk-sharing places too much of a burden on the working class, but workers and wage-earners already bear the risks of business failures and economic downturns through unemployment—they just don't get paid for it. Most wage contracts, such as those negotiated by unions, do not reduce risk but merely transfer it, usually from the politically strongest to the weakest. We see this trend in two-tier union wage contracts where senior members retain benefits that new members will not receive. In a fluid capitalist economy, it is becoming apparent that wage contracts are low-risk, low-return strategies that reduce the ability of workers to get paid for risk and to share in the returns to success. The specter of wage competition from the expanding international supply of labor should be warning enough that the rules of the game have changed.

There is one last principle of policy design that we must add:

5. **As uncertainty reduces the level of economic risk-taking, our public policies should strive to reduce the uncertainty associated with economic decisions. This means that government policy directives should be clear, transparent, consistent, and far-sighted. A firm commitment to first principles helps insure this outcome.**

The essential action of life in a free market economy in an uncertain world is *risk-taking*. Our strategies to survive in this world involve managing the inherent risks we face in order to take additional risks of our choosing. If someone has several million dollars in the bank, he or she may then feel comfortable to pursue the financially precarious life of an artist or intellectual. If someone has a broad job skill set, he or she may be more inclined to start up a new business in a chosen field. These strategies we pursue at the individual, or microeconomic, level should be enhanced, not constrained or hampered, by our public policies. A good example of how policy constrains risk-taking is linking health insurance to places of employment, with the result that many people stay in a job merely because they fear losing affordable insurance. This fear greatly impairs entrepreneurial risk-taking. In an uncertain world, we should strive to make sure our policies do not increase that uncertainty unnecessarily.

To summarize, let us restate the preceding five principles of policy design:

1. Economic policy and politics should serve the principles of freedom; in the realm of public policy this translates into maximizing *freedom of choice* and *freedom of action*.

2. Policies should facilitate the flexibility of the economy, improving its

adaptability to unpredictable change. Thus, policies should facilitate the fluid reallocation of resources. This requires accurate price signals provided by competitive markets.

3. To facilitate change, public policies should primarily focus on managing risk, either through helping citizens manage their own risks, establishing laws that ensure competitive private insurance markets, or providing social insurance.

    i. The preferred policy for risk management is self-insurance through increased savings and diversified asset holdings;

    ii. The next policy priority should be to support efficient private insurance markets;

    iii. In cases of insurance market incompleteness or failure, policy should resort to universal social insurance systems funded by taxed contributions; ideally, these contributions can be based on expected losses as determined by actuarial data.

4. Capital is the lifeblood of a free market society. Economic and tax policies should promote capital accumulation and widespread participation in capital ownership.

5. Because uncertainty reduces the level of economic risk-taking, our public policies should strive to reduce the uncertainty associated with economic decisions. This means government policy directives should be clear, transparent, consistent and far-sighted.

Guided by these policy principles, we will apply our understanding of the economy to several of our most challenging policy issues.

CHAPTER FIVE

The Main Policy Challenges

We could spend an entire book analyzing all the ways we fall short of first principles in formulating economic and social policy. Instead, I will focus on the main challenges we face today. These are Federal Reserve policy and banking reform, fiscal reform, tax reform, entitlement reform, and the principal-agent problem.

5.1 Federal Reserve Policy

The Federal Reserve was established in 1913 in order to manage the private banking system and avoid panics that were common to the 19th century. The 1913 Act has been amended over the years, expanding the Fed's original purpose and mandate. Currently, the two principal functions that concern our policy discussion are:

1. Managing the nation's money supply to achieve the sometimes-conflicting goals of
   a. Stable prices, including prevention of either inflation or deflation
   b. Maximum employment
   c. Moderate long-term interest rates
2. Maintain the stability of the financial system and contain *systemic risk* in financial markets by regulating member banks.

We already discussed how the money supply is manipulated through credit creation by the fractional-reserve banking system under the imperfect control of the Fed. In 1946, the Full Employment Act introduced an additional policy objective of promoting full employment for the Federal Reserve. Today, the twin goals of price stability *and* full employment (1.a and 1.b above) are referred to as the Fed's "dual mandate." These goals conflict, however, when the choice is between lowering interest rates to stimulate investment and employment versus raising interest rates to tighten the money supply and dampen inflation pressures. The conflict is easily politicized because politicians facing re-election favor short-term stimulus spending to increase employment over long term price stability. Excessive public and private debts have also tilted the balance between inflation and deflation in favor of inflation. Knowledge of these policy biases has fostered uncertainty and investor anxiety over the future value of the dollar, as well as the policy direction of a Fed faced with conflicting goals.

Recent results of monetary policy, combined with the logic of our model, suggests policymakers may be pursuing a false trade-off between employment and price stability with wrong-headed policies that deliver neither. Let's investigate this possibility.

We must remember that neither the Federal Reserve nor the government directly 'creates' employment and production. It is the private economy that creates jobs through business expansion and entrepreneurial start-ups. In order for the private economy to expand, businesses need to understand their own financial risks relative to the future value of the dollar and government policies that may affect the expected future value of their investments.

We often hear from the politicians that their main priority is "jobs, jobs, and jobs," but what does that really mean in practice? Public spending can be employed toward this goal by creating positive externalities that help the private sector become more productive. For example, Congress can authorize to build a road as a public good, paid for with taxpayer money. The government does not collect any revenue from the road, which is used by private parties to reduce transportation costs and broaden markets. Thus, the private sector expands as a result of this public spending externality. (This assumes that the road would not be provided by the for-profit, private sector. If it was, there would be no need for the government to step in.)

However, if the government spends money on activities that either create no positive externalities or that substitute for private sector businesses, the spending represents a mere substitution of public for private investment. No gain in production or employment results and the administrative costs represent a welfare loss to the economy. Let us consider another example to demonstrate. The government decides to hire one crew of workers to dig a ditch and then another crew to fill in the ditch. All are fully employed digging and filling in ditches and everybody gets paid a decent wage, say $20/hour plus benefits. There is no real production to show for all this effort, but each worker now has more money to buy food, clothing, etc. Is this a positive externality? Probably not. Let's imagine a private developer wished to employ these same workers to build low cost housing, but could only pay $15/hour with fewer benefits. But the labor resources he needs are unavailable, soaked up by the non-productive government sector. The net effect to the economy is a loss of productive jobs and income growth.

This example illustrates how public investment, absorbing labor and capital resources, can "crowd out" private sector activity that would lead to greater job growth and production. Perhaps this sounds theoretical, but what exactly was "Cash for Clunkers"? It was a policy that destroyed assets (older cars) in order to subsidize the purchase of newer, more expensive assets (fuel-efficient cars). All this did was subsidize car purchases that would have occurred but were moved forward in time to take advantage of the price break. The policy also removed used cars from the market that many buyers who could not afford a new car would have liked to purchase and use. If one wants to grow an economy, this policy makes little sense. (Of course, we should realize this was a political gambit to save jobs in the auto industry – jobs that eventually may disappear anyway.)

In Chapters Two and Three we discussed the importance of the interest rate and predictable currency values for stable, sustainable economic growth. Unfortunately, the dual mandate forces the Fed to manipulate interest rates, compromising its mission of price stability and distorting crucial price signals that guide consumers, savers, borrowers, and investors. All sorts of sleights of hand have been employed to try to obscure this fact with rosier headline economic statistics (see previous discussion on government statistics). We should also raise questions about the actual results of such policies. The president's Council of Economic Advisors recently calculated that only 2.4 million new jobs could be directly attributed to $666 billion of government stimulus spending. The cost to taxpayers comes to $278,000 per job! Due to generous rules for counting new jobs, that figure is probably vastly understated. It's difficult to defend this sort of public investment policy.

Given the obvious limitations of government to affect employment directly, it would probably be better policy if the Fed focused solely on ensuring the purchasing power of the dollar so the private economy could adjust to stable, undistorted prices. The less uncertainty businesses face, the more confidence they will have to make risk-taking investments in the future. The alternative, which we are experiencing now, has burdened us with idle capital and underinvestment, asset speculation, underemployment, undercapacity, and anemic real growth, to say nothing of the future implications of exploding public debt.

The next issue on the Fed's policy agenda is the problem of managing the banking system and controlling systemic risk. The root of this challenge can be found in a financial system dominated by credit creation and debt. Debt, as opposed to equity (or stock), increases and concentrates risk. It does this through financial leverage and legal contractual obligations. When a business issues stock, the investors assume the risk of loss to the limit of the investment, without any guarantees. When business obtains a loan from a bank, or issues a bond, it assumes a legal contract under the loan terms specifying the right of the lenders to be repaid ahead of other claimants, such as equity investors. Lenders also have first claim on the salvage value of any assets owned by the business, such as plant and machinery, real estate, or inventory. The finance term for this priority is seniority, so debt finance is senior to equity finance. This is why equity investors are often called residual claimants, meaning they can claim any profit residuals *only after* every other liability of the business is paid off. Technically, they are also the owners of the business, which is why they are called shareholders and stocks are called shares.

From the point of view of the business, debt obligations concentrate the risks of the business onto the owners of the business, while equity finance spreads the business risk by creating new ownership rights. Since equity investors assume more risk, they also expect higher returns if the business is successful. With business success, equity finance can be quite expensive to the business owner, or entrepreneur, because he or she had to give up ownership rights and residual claims to profits. These higher returns demanded by equity investors are the business owner's trade-off for more financial flexibility. If the business suffers losses, equity investors share those losses, whereas lenders and debt holders still have legal recourse to interest and principal payments. If debts are not serviced or repaid, the business can be forced into bankruptcy where its assets are liquidated to pay off as much debt as possible. This means a business funded by debt has less flexibility to adapt to unexpected market shocks.

An entire financial system that depends primarily on debt finance is going to present greater risks of a systemic collapse. Fundamentally, this is why the losses of the dot-com crash were more easily absorbed by the economy than the losses of the housing crash. When dot-com companies' stocks crashed, unsecured equity, or "funny money," disappeared. Dot.com bubble gains felt surreal, like Monopoly money, with the mere illusion of value. In contrast, when the housing market crashed and house prices fell, mortgages still have to be paid in full, putting a crushing burden on those who borrowed excessively with the expectation that prices always go up. With the integration of credit through securitized collateralized debt obligations, the chain reaction of defaults spread far and wide. The U.S. crisis of subprime mortgages quickly became a crisis that threatened the entire worldwide financial system.

The Federal Reserve's mandate to regulate and stabilize the banking system to contain systemic risk is severely compromised by the rise of a worldwide shadow banking system. The expansion of finance, worldwide integration of financial markets, and the lack of sovereign government control over multinational banking means that many of the tools that governments use to regulate the banking system are obsolete and ineffective. Leading up to the crisis, unregulated, non-banking entities such as investment banks (Bear Stearns, Lehman, Goldman Sachs, Morgan Stanley), hedge funds, foreign banks, and private companies like AIG issued billions of dollars of highly leveraged credit. The potential failure of these 'shadow banks' led to cries of "too big to fail" and the eventual TARP[62] bailouts.

The Fed has embraced its easy credit policy in a desperate attempt to get the economy back on track. But it's still the wrong track. Subsidized interest rates have hurt savers and creditors, and rewarded marginal borrowers, asset speculators, and consumers. One former hedge fund manager, assessing the Fed's management of the crisis, commented: "Just don't forget that zero interest rates are not real—they are a construct of the Fed, not the market, and they are dangerously distorting the crucial capital-allocation process."

In order to get monetary policy back on track, we should narrow the mission of the monetary authorities and enforce some stability into the policymaking process through transparency and accountability. Instead we have gone in the opposite direction by granting the Federal Reserve and the U.S. Treasury extraordinary discretion over our economic future. This should not have been necessary. Consider these statements made by our present Federal Reserve chairman Ben Bernanke in the run-up to the worst financial crisis since the 1930s:

> "We've never had a decline in house prices on a nationwide basis. So, what I think what is more likely is that house prices will slow, maybe stabilize" (July 1, 2005).

> "...the impact on the broader economy and financial markets of the problems in the subprime markets seems likely to be contained" (March 28, 2007).

> [Freddie Mac and Fannie Mae] "will make it through the storm" [and are] "adequately capitalized" (July 16, 2008).

As one policy wag put it, Bernanke has been wrong with his financial predictions more often than the weatherman! But this is no laughing matter. Our credit-driven monetary management over the past twenty-five years has turned the relationship between the financial service sector and the real economy on its head. We have essentially created a financial market casino, where the banking industry lays bets on price movements of financial and real assets instead of making long-term loans to businesses. Price volatility is a Wall Street gambler's best friend and easy credit policies have grossly distorted prices of everything—from houses, to securities, to gold and commodities, to final goods and services.

The subsequent loss of confidence in the U.S. financial system and the Federal Reserve's mismanagement of the banking system imposes real costs on the domestic economy. These real costs lie behind the price bubbles and busts that have misinformed our economic decisions, causing us to make the wrong consumption, saving, and investment decisions, misallocating the deployment of scarce resources that ensures the long run sustainability of the economy. Our savings have been inadequate, our borrowing excessive, and our investment and production misdirected. In simple terms, we've spent too much money on houses, automobiles, and other discretionary goods sold at the mall, and spent too little on food, pensions, energy production, and other necessities.

The increased money creation discretion of central bankers has had its positive benefits in helping to develop private capital markets, increasing access to capital for a wider range of investors, and funding economic growth around the world. But the desire to stimulate investment with low interest rates means we have been subsidizing excessive credit borrowing as the main source of investment. Fractional reserve banking amplifies credit bubbles through the leveraging of debt. The massive reliance on debt has had a profound effect on the riskiness of the system and how that risk is distributed.

In the end, we face a conundrum. We have developed a financial system that depends on credit creation and debt assumption with the consequence that it has become more far more prone to market volatility and systemic risk. Ironically, the results defy the fundamental logic and purpose of financial markets to diversify and manage risk prudently. We truly need to think outside the box we've put ourselves in. Let us consider some policy proposals suggested by our simple analytical model.

1. The Federal Reserve should be tasked solely with defending the purchasing power of the currency and monitoring and regulating the health of the commercial banking system. While Fed policy should assume close political oversight, policy should be driven by price rules that constrain interest rate distortions and insulate the goal of price stability from political interference.

The regulation of the banking system requires two correctives.

2. With every reward comes the risk of failure. If a business entity should become "too big to fail," it is *too big to exist* with a government guarantee. We should allow large corporations to discover their most efficient scale and diversified product mix. The promise of market success, however, must come with the discipline imposed by possible market failure. Otherwise, we risk the devastating costs of moral hazard. They say nothing concentrates the mind like the prospect of a hanging, and the economic equivalent of a hanging is bankruptcy. The sanction of bankruptcy is crucial to controlling the risks of the shadow-banking industry.

3. Fed policy should monitor and dampen excess debt leverage in the fractional-banking credit creation process. Financial debt bubbles are fueled by excessive leverage. We need to rethink and reform tax policies that favor debt over equity finance.

(This issue will be more fully addressed in the tax policy section that follows.)

Even though financial innovation, capital market development and integration has given us stronger and broader economic growth, easy central bank policy through discretionary credit creation has saddled us with volatile capital markets and wrenching economic adjustments. Our policy responses have been driven by the imperatives of campaign politics and accommodative monetary policy, directly affecting the long-term health of our national economy and our own individual life prospects. This is how financial policy has become the tail that wags the dog of international economic performance.

5.2 Fiscal Reform

We have addressed fiscal policy in reference to government stimulus spending, exploding public debt, and the incentives facing politicians. Fiscal policy and monetary policy are two sides of the same coin, so we cannot reform one without the other. As discussed in the section on Financial Alchemy, the Fed and the government are operating on either end of the credit creation—debt issuance equation. If the government spends beyond its means, then the Fed's mandate to maintain full employment and price stability will force it to find ways to fund the government debt. In the US, total Federal government debt has grown from $10 trillion to over $14 trillion in the last two years alone. Under current budget projections this debt is expected to grow by $1-2 trillion per year for the next ten years. By facilitating credit creation with easy monetary policies, the Fed is enabling profligate public spending. In simple words, we Americans are living beyond our financial means, while the Fed is in the compromised position of signing off on our checks.

If we want the Fed to adopt sound monetary principles, we will have to reform the budgetary process and seek ways to restrain government deficit spending. Unfortunately, because of the arcana of public finance and monetary policy, the need to control spending has been the source of a great deal of misinformation. As of 2011, the major political issue has become the federal debt limit and the projection of future government deficits that will place an unsupportable debt burden on future generations. This may well carry forward into the 2012 presidential election cycle. But, because we are now in a fiat currency regime, we are focusing on the wrong measures. The overall debt limit is now a distraction—uncomfortable perhaps, but still a distraction. Instead, we need to consider the long–term consequences of excess debt on the productive capacity of the U.S. and world economy. This is better measured by the ratio of total debt to GDP. In addition, we can measure the short-term trend with the ratio of the annual deficit to GDP. This ratio shows whether our spending is having the positive effect of increasing our incomes, wealth, and standard of living, or merely impoverishing us in the long term.

The imperative to live within our budgetary means is illuminated by our model—not because we cannot carry the debt, but because budgetary constraints force us to set public priorities and choose prudent policies. Due to debt creation, we, as a nation, have been financing future growth with debt rather than through the difficult trade-offs between present and deferred consumption. This has created excess current consumption as well as excess investment for future consumption. Based on exploding credit creation and debt obligations, this trend is unsustainable. In the private sector, our post-financial crisis economy has been correcting through drastic financial de-leveraging in order to repair balance sheets. At a personal level, this means reducing debt to the level where we can service it out of current income. The difference between personal and public finance, however, is that the government can accumulate debts and never go bankrupt (see footnote #13); it is only required to service its payment commitments by collecting taxes or issuing new debt. Whereas the prospect of financial insolvency restrains our personal borrowing, there is no such restraint on the public purse.

There are several possible policy reforms to restrain budgetary deficits. One is a balanced budget amendment to the Constitution. This would require the Federal government to balance its budget much like the fifty states are required to do now. There are two counterarguments to a balanced amendment. First, it would reduce the flexibility of the government to adapt fiscal policy to changing economic conditions, such as the recent financial and banking crisis. Second, it might also feed a desire to raise taxes to maintain or increase spending levels. A different approach would be to restrict government expenditures to a certain percentage of the prior year's GDP, say 18-20%. Flexibility could be enhanced by allowing temporary departures that would require compensating reductions in future budgets, so that any excess spending in one year would require spending reductions in subsequent years until the budget was back in balance and the outstanding debts repaid. In any policy, greater transparency and Congressional accountability over the budgetary process is necessary.

All budgetary reforms are dependent on tax revenue issues and tax policy, which we turn to next.

5.3 Tax Reform

Tax policy should be guided by how we answer two basic questions. The first question asks how much in tax revenues are needed to fund desired public goods and services. The second question asks how do we fairly and efficiently obtain, or collect, those needed revenues.

The objective of tax policy *should* be to achieve exactly the correct amount of revenues needed to fund the public budget. If we desire military protection, security against crime, functioning roads, streetlights, etc., citizens need to contribute taxes in one form or another to pay for these public goods. Naturally, our political battles rage over the levels of public goods and services government needs to provide and the most fair and efficient method to fund these needs. (Regrettably, efficiency is usually the last criterion to be considered.)

So, to answer the first question requires us to distinguish between public and private goods and services. We can hardly expect, or want, the government to provide everything we need in life. First, because of the lack of profit motives and price signals, the public sector is often less efficient than the private sector. Goods socially provided are usually inferior in quality and cost more. If they cost less, it is usually because of subsidies, and the supply is rationed, so the real cost is much higher. (Keep this in mind when discussing public health care and the possibility of getting a heart transplant.) Second, the government as sole or primary provider constitutes a quasi-monopoly that constrains the freedoms and choices that a diversified private market offers. We discussed the differences between public and private goods in Chapter Two in the section on Market Failures.

To answer the second question concerning efficiency and fairness, we need to apply what we know about economic behavior and psychology. The tax system offers the most promising realm for economic policy impact because taxes most directly affect individual behavior by altering the basic risk-return calculation that governs our economic decisions. If we calculate an acceptable expected return from a risky venture and the government taxes that return at 40%, tax policy will alter the entire risk-return trade-off. The more taxes distort economic incentives, the more prices will be distorted in the market, yielding greater misallocation of resources. For this reason, most economists advocate taxes that have the least measurable impact on economic decisions. In other words, they desire tax effects to be neutral. If we tax income too high, for example, people will produce less by diverting their efforts to satisfying activities that can't be taxed, such as leisure time. In this way, higher tax rates will yield fewer tax revenues. This was the basis of the supply-side revolution of the 1980s. Of course, if tax rates are too low, tax revenues and public services will suffer. The goal is to identify the ideal tax rate that maximizes revenue. Unfortunately, arguments over taxes become politicized to justify whatever objective is desired, such as less or more government spending, tax preferences for favored constituencies, social engineering, or expanding bureaucratic power.

In 2008, in developed countries, the total tax revenues as a share of the economy as measured by GDP ranged from a low of 21% to a high of 48%, averaging out to 35%. In the U.S., the range over the past fifty years has been between 24% and 29%, with recent levels around 28%. Of course, when government spending exceeds tax receipts, we get annual deficits that accumulate to total outstanding government debt. The total debts of these countries ranges from 5% to 178% of GDP, the U.S. was last at 60% headed for 80%. Over 100% is considered the danger zone, but these static numbers tell us little as it is the direction in which a country's finances are headed that really matters. The annual deficit as a share of GDP is a good indicator, but the real focus must be on the economic viability of fiscal and tax policy. The concept is not much different than with personal household finances. If wages and incomes are rising and spending increases at a slower rate, debts can be paid off. This means that maximizing the economic growth rate is an important objective of tax policy, and tax policy, in turn, can have a significant effect on that growth rate.

If we consult our economic model, we understand that we should seek the optimal growth rate consistent with sustainability, as opposed to the maximum growth rate. We should be pacing ourselves like a marathon runner rather than trying to race like a sprinter—the destination is the same, but it matters how you get there. The tricky part is that because the optimal rate is a product of accurate price signals that tell us how much to consume, save, invest, and produce, we cannot choose the optimal growth rate in advance and then choose policies to make it happen. The best we can do is to permit the economy to adjust to these price signals with a minimum of distortion or market disruption.

Given the various incentives surrounding the formulation of tax policy, we need to incorporate certain guiding principles to keep policy from being hijacked by narrow interests. Our first principle is:

1. **Since taxes are needed to pay for public goods, all goods and services that can be provided by the private economy should not be commandeered by politics and provided less efficiently by the public sector.**

We need to insure that our fiscal budgets are not overburdened unnecessarily. This does not preclude the fact that certain markets and private industries may require regulatory oversight and legal enforcement. What many ideologues will find objectionable here is the unarguable fact that healthcare and retirement are private, not public, goods. We will address this in the next section on entitlement reform. Our second principle is:

2. **A growing economy increases tax revenues, so tax policy should seek to impose the least amount of distortion over economic decisions, especially those of people on the frontline of risk-taking behavior.**

Unfortunately this is the principle we violate most egregiously. Different taxes affect economic choices differently. We have taxes on income, we have taxes on retail sales, and we have taxes on property and inheritances. We can categorize these respectively as taxes on production, consumption, and wealth. We have a propensity to tax productive activities, which means these taxes (on wages, incomes, business profits, capital gains) weigh upon investment risk-return decisions before the fact, decreasing investment and channeling it into less productive, but lesser taxed activities. To put it simply, taxes on production are counter-productive.

The most neutral taxes are taxes on consumption (sales or use taxes, value-added taxes or VAT). This logically flows from our initial economic decree that all economic decisions can be reduced to the decision to consume now or later. A consumption tax, imposed either today or tomorrow, has little effect on that time-sensitive decision to consume. Either we pay the same tax today or the same tax tomorrow, the tax does not change our preference for when we choose to consume. Thus, the tax's effect is neutral. We may defer consumption, but that won't reduce the tax. However, when we tax production we affect the decision of whether to consume now or later since we reduce the amount we can expect to consume later relative to today. When we tax productive activity we get less saving, less investment, and more present consumption. All other things equal, this reduces economic growth. Remember, we only produce in order to affect our consumption levels over time.

A wealth tax is less distorting than an income tax, though not as neutral as a consumption tax. A property tax serves to pay for those public goods associated with landed property or real estate, such as roads, utilities, police and fire security, street lighting, etc. An inheritance tax is often justified in terms of fairness, as it counters the accumulation of economic and political power in a single family over generations, even though the production of that wealth has already been taxed.

Taxes on productive activity (which is any activity that increases wealth, in material or non-material terms) have a negative impact on several of the policy objectives we outlined previously. The distortions introduced by productive taxes directly impact the calculations of risk and return, raising the hurdle rate for investment.[63] More seriously, taxes on production reduce savings and capital accumulation that can serve to insure against the risk of losses. The propensity of politicians to manipulate income taxes for political reasons also increases the overall level of uncertainty in the economy, reducing productive risk-taking. Because businesses and individuals cannot accurately forecast after-tax profits, they postpone or cut investment. As opposed to "the rich," these risk-takers are the most productive members of society. The overall effect is to tax the "getting" of wealth more than the "having" of wealth. By targeting the most productive members of society, we also harm most the neediest people in society who depend on job growth. This is inconsistent with our constitutional principles of freedom and providing equal opportunity, unnecessarily creating class tensions between the rich and the poor.

We must also consider that any tax regime must compete in a global market and this is particularly critical with regard to taxes on labor and capital. Taxes on wages (payroll taxes) can make U.S. workers uncompetitive with foreign workers at comparable skill levels. Of course, labor productivity is a function of how we combine labor with capital, but since capital must also compete on the world market, taxes on production disadvantage both domestic labor and capital. Free market competition and the mobility of capital means we need to create the most efficient tax system given the constraints of world markets. We need to meet this objective in order to create a fair tax system. A corporate income tax has two pernicious effects: it makes domestic companies less competitive on the world market, and it encourages political patronage for corporate welfare by creating an incentive to lobby for favorable treatment to reduce tax burdens or shift the taxes to competitors. A VAT tax that substitutes for the corporate income tax would eliminate both these distortions, while still collecting the necessary revenues.

A tax system that relies wholly on consumption taxes would not work ideally because it encourages black markets and cross-border smuggling of consumption goods on a mass scale. It would suffice to find a balance between various sources of revenue, with a minimum of economic distortion. A flat income tax that greatly broadens the tax base would help to simplify the tax code while removing much of the political favoritism for narrow interests.

One particular distortion that has aggravated our recent financial crisis is the differential treatment between equity and debt capital. We allow the expensing of interest payments on debt for corporations and household mortgage debt, which has served to subsidize debt by making it cheaper. In the case of corporations, tax rules favoring debt have tilted financing preferences toward debt away from equity. Excessive corporate debt has several deleterious side effects. It increases and concentrates risk by reducing the financial flexibility of the firm, increasing its financial leverage, and concentrating ownership and the returns to ownership through leverage. When a firm obtains new finance through debt, the existing ownership is merely leveraged by that debt without creating any new equity investors. This means the increased profits accrue to the same owners.

The trend toward excessive debt leverage is probably due more to the Fed's implied support of credit markets over the past 25 years than tax policy. If the Fed is going to bail out bad debts, the trade-offs between equity and debt become a one-way bet for existing owners and management. The incentive for corporate business is to load up on cheap debt and gamble the capital on risky projects. It's another case of "heads we win, tails the taxpayer loses." The capital financing decisions of firms should reflect the risks facing the firm and the optimal ownership structure of the firm and industry, not its tax advantages as determined by political motives or moral hazard engendered by Fed policy.

In the case of homeowners, the mortgage deduction has increased the debt loads for all real estate mortgages by raising the purchase prices of home. Because interest payments are tax-deductible, mortgages are subsidized by tax deductions. But this just causes house prices to rise as people can afford to borrow and pay more. So, the money we save with interest deductions is more than offset by the increased principal amounts we must borrow to buy the house! Home owners now have higher debt loads and less equity, meaning they are less able to absorb price declines and less able to convert equity to debt in times of trouble. Tax policy that favors debt over equity helps leverage risk, but also reduces the adaptability of the economy to change. With debt we get more risk and less flexibility. The results of excessive debt in the real estate sector speak for themselves.

My last principle flows from the objective to distribute the risks and benefits of wealth creation:

3. **Tax policy should reinforce the objective of risk management through the diversification of risk and the widespread accumulation of returns. The imperative to participate in capitalism through equity should be promoted, not impeded.**

Our most intractable economic problems are those of maldistribution. Misguided tax policy has done much to aggravate these problems and contribute to the divergence of incomes and wealth. For example, if savings and capital accumulation help spread the benefits of economic growth and enable citizens to more efficiently insure against risks, why do we tax dividends, savings, and capital gains at both the corporate and individual level? Why not remove these taxes completely for middle and low-income levels? Why do we place such onerous restrictions on tax-free accounts for retirement, health care, and education, when these private funds can directly reduce the burden on social insurance and public goods provision? Why do we punish savings with a monetary policy that keeps interest rates so low?

Inequality has been blamed on a host of factors, mostly targeting the indifferent or conspiratorial rich, but, as I have argued, I believe most income disparities can be attributed to technology and the changes it has wrought. The global winner-take-all economy cannot really be blamed on the winners, but it does demand a policy corrective in some form (such as a wealth tax). Whatever form this corrective takes, it will surely incite a resurgence of conflict between those who stand to win and those who stand to lose. If we do not provide the corrective, however, the economy will become chronically unstable and we will all likely suffer in one way or another. A class crisis either takes the form of a political revolution or an economic and social disaster. It would be better if the problem were addressed with a deliberate and principled strategy that does not condemn us to an endless pendulum swing from one policy to its opposite.

5.4 Risk, Insurance, and Entitlements

As discussed previously, the management of economic risk and uncertainty is one of the primary functions of a democratic society. Our attempts to manage risk through Social Security, Medicare, Medicaid, and other social insurance programs, such as unemployment and state disability, have proven to be neither optimal nor efficient. On the other hand, the private market for these goods has been found wanting and distorted by government regulation and intervention. The conventional defense of social insurance programs deems that they have been found to be necessary. The need and demand for economic security is real, but the methods for providing it offer a wide array of policy choices. The opposition to, and difficulties enacting, entitlement reform are mostly political in nature. Loss aversion dictates that we cannot eliminate program benefits without providing a more suitable substitute for participants who have planned on these benefits. In discussing economic security and entitlement reform, the first caveat to consider is that there is no free lunch. What I mean is that economic security, whether provided as a public or private good, is not free—our choices involve trade-offs. The basic trade-off is over who controls the rationing of scarce healthcare and old-age benefits: the individual or the state? I will argue here that a wise combination of the two is the best solution.

We have previously explained in Chapter Two why self-insurance is superior to private insurance, which is superior to social insurance, under the explicit objectives of risk management. We face an additional challenge with our entitlement programs because they are not really insurance pools. They are pay-as-you-go transfer systems (PAYG), which present a host of financial problems.

First, the PAYG system does not save and reap the benefits of interest compounding, so there is no true "investment return" on Social Security or Medicare contributions. Second, because funds paid in by workers are immediately paid out to beneficiaries, the system relies on demographic dependency ratios. Presently, there are three workers paying into the system for each beneficiary. Within twenty years that ratio will fall to 2 to 1, implying that the taxes on every two workers will have to be enough to completely support one retiree. Third, redistributive programs exact high moral hazard costs by creating disincentives for saving, depressing national savings for productive investment, and depriving people of the necessary incentives to economize on healthcare.

We must dispel the fear invoked by the idea that these programs can or will go bankrupt. There is no debt constraint on the U.S. Treasury when it comes to paying off dollar liabilities, so any obligations of the U.S.

government will be paid without question. Instead, we should be worried about the U.S. economy's ability to create the goods and services that retirees need to purchase. If the economy does not supply these in abundance, prices will skyrocket and entitlement benefits will be inadequate. The danger comes from imprudent social insurance programs that do not pay for themselves over time and soak up valuable resources from other productive segments of the economy. So, it goes without saying that these programs need to be reformed and rationalized to economic and financial realities. Social Security is the easier fix it makes perfect sense to raise the retirement age and perhaps means-test benefits. Benefit calculations can also be adjusted to reflect real cost of living changes.

With publicly-subsidized healthcare there are no market incentives to restrain the primary cost drivers. Think about it: we have removed the negative feedback processes we discussed earlier that help keep goods markets in equilibrium. The hospital, drug company, or doctor can raise prices, but that does nothing to depress demand because the patient never sees or pays the price directly. The reality is that there are no real, posted prices. Imagine going into a supermarket where there are no prices on the goods, and when you get to the checkout, you're given a total bill for $5000 dollars for your basket of groceries! (Or maybe the supermarket will bill you a month later, after you've eaten all the food, just to avoid riots at the cash register.) If we expect a market to work, all participants must have access to accurate price signals in order to make efficient choices. (The airline industry may need to take this cue too.)

The better long-term strategy to mitigate the shortcomings of entitlement programs is to substitute self-insurance and private insurance markets for the bulk of entitlement needs. We have already covered the difference between private and public goods here. Private goods are provided in abundance by private markets—just visit your local grocery or department store. Similar private market options can be provided with regard to both retirement and healthcare needs. This, despite the fact that democratic governments around the world have responded to citizen demands to make these public goods. If we choose to have government provide these goods while restraining the private market, there is no escaping the fact that they will be delivered less efficiently and there will be less to distribute. In order to provide a good, it must first be produced, and the public sector does not efficiently produce or distribute goods. Granted, this is one of the more controversial issues in our current politics, because our political efforts to convert these private goods to public goods through excessive regulation have distorted supply and demand, hampering private markets. We must rationalize private markets so they function efficiently in providing for the needs of our population. We already provide for most of our retirement needs with private pension plans, private health insurance, and a slew of individual investment plans such as Health Savings Accounts, IRAs and 410(k)s. These should be expanded, with flexible rules that meet the needs of participants, not those of the tax collectors or bureaucratic administrators.

Medical care has been provided privately for almost the entire history of the U.S. There is no defensible argument that we now need public provision. The bottom line is that if we want first rate medical care as a nation, we will have to save enough and invest in the R&D and production of that care. As with Social Security, the problem is not *how do we pay for it*, but *how do we insure a sufficient supply of goods and services demanded*. At the individual level, we need to make the proper savings decisions to assume the bulk of our healthcare needs. There is no way government can deliver such goods out of thin air. Inadequate provision of healthcare goods and services means an undersupply that, with central control of the production and delivery, must be rationed by supply instead of price. This inescapable fact of rationing invites all kinds of arbitrary decision rules about 'who gets what' that violates our first principle of policymaking: to insure freedom of choice and freedom of action. To truly solve our healthcare needs we need functioning competitive markets, with real prices, so we may compare and choose from many choices in order to make rational decisions on how to best secure our long-term health while maintaining financial solvency. A rational market in healthcare goods will efficiently provide the goods we demand at the prices we are willing to pay. Then we can tweak the distribution of this abundance of healthcare goods without killing the golden goose that lays the eggs. In addition, we need a functioning insurance market that allows us to insure against unpredictable catastrophic healthcare contingencies. Nothing mentioned in the recent Patient Protection and Affordable Care Act (*aka* Obamacare) seems to come close to meeting these needs.

5.5 The Principal-Agent Problem

The *principal-agent problem* is an opaque issue that is not often discussed outside of economics. Markets, especially financial markets and democratic political markets, rely heavily on "agents" in order to function efficiently and effectively. An agent in this sense is nothing more than someone who executes a service for you in your interest. Our elected politicians and local city councils are agents, so are the managers and the Boards of Directors of the businesses where we work, or the bankers who manage our savings. The teachers who teach our kids are agents, as are the union leaders who represent teachers' interests. The President of the United States is an agent who is sworn to uphold the Constitution and represent the interests of U.S. citizens in world affairs. The person or persons whose interest is being represented by the agent is called the principal. The principal-agent conflict is a general and pervasive one: how can we insure that agents act in the interests of their principals and not in their own self-interests, which may conflict with those of their principals?

This is no trivial matter. If an elected politician violates his campaign promises, our only recourse is to throw him or her out in the next election. If our banker takes imprudent risks with our savings, we may discover unexpected losses of those savings. And if the CEO of a public company misuses shareholder funds, we may discover our investment has been misappropriated. We've been cheated, even when it is done within the letter of the law.

There is no way to completely eliminate agency costs, just as there is no way to eliminate moral hazard in insurance pools. The best we can do is to *align incentives* between principal and agent, require *transparency*, and *monitor* and *sanction* agent behavior to minimize violations of the public trust. When it comes to controlling agent behavior, proper incentives are often more effective than regulations, as laws are easily subverted, while monitoring and enforcing compliance can be extremely costly. We cannot just pass a law, put a police officer on every corner, and expect good results. The agency costs that inflict the most damage on our society are those associated with corporate ownership and control, organized labor, financial markets, democratic politics, and the bureaucracy.

In democratic politics we have established a constitutional structure of checks and balances to guard against the concentration of political power and reduce the potential for governmental abuse. But even in a democracy we can see the after-effects of backroom deals, the power of incumbency (when those in power make the rules), and politicians' persistent efforts to obscure the truth. Certainly transparency and accountability are critical to the democratic political process and often are the only means to expose political malfeasance. The traditional media, which has now been supplemented by alternative media, is tasked to perform this function. This is one reason why the overt politicization of media can be a detriment to a free society, as biased information either misleads or is ignored.

Beyond legal monitoring and judicial enforcement, we ultimately must rely on voters to control agents' behavior in a democracy. True electoral competition is democracy's saving grace, as rigged elections are its nemesis. Removing electoral barriers that favor incumbents can motivate candidates to restrain their own behavior while policing others. In other words, viable challengers are driven to keep an eye on incumbents' actions in office and inform voters of any malfeasance.

In economic markets, we must also be mindful of how incentives operate through checks and balances. The checks and balances are provided by market competition and the "voters" are consumers, shareholders, and other enterprise stakeholders, such as workers and creditors. The major agency problem in the private sector has always been over how to govern the public corporation. In public companies, shareholders provide capital through equity ownership and then rely on managers and directors to act in their interests. This particular agency relationship invites conflicts of interest between managers and directors, and a lack of transparency for shareholders. Managers often appoint directors, who then pass judgment on managerial decisions such as executive compensation and perks. As the board of directors of a public company is meant to represent shareholders, this cozy relationship with management presents a conflict of interest.

The costs of monitoring directors or organizing and fighting management are often too great given shareholders' small ownership interests. If management is violating small shareholders' interests, it makes more sense to sell and move on. This *collective action problem* causes shareholders to manage their investment risks by diversifying their ownership interests across many different public companies. But this diversification strategy leaves a vacuum of control, with no one to rein in corporate management, creating incentives for mismanagement and inefficiency throughout the corporate business sector.

In order for market capitalism to work efficiently, while promoting wider ownership participation for all, *corporate governance* issues must be managed and minimized, and collective action problems must be resolved. One route is to impose independent directors elected by shareholders rather than appointed by management. Another has been to pass laws that ensure managers and directors are accountable to shareholders. Securities markets have long required adherence to reporting and accounting standards for publicly listed companies. Still, this hasn't been enough to defend shareholder ownership.

We might go further by applying a democratic political model in certain aspects. Like universal suffrage in democratic politics, democratic capitalism requires universal participation in risk-taking enterprise through stakeholder ownership. Stakeholders include not only shareholders and management, but also workers, suppliers, and customers. The most effective way to internalize the principal-agent problem among these various stakeholders is through equity participation in ownership. Ownership assumes the risks of loss as well as rewards of success.

Likewise, the consequences of ownership also imply the exercise of *control* over the risks and rewards. (Owners are risk-takers, and no skydiver wants to risk jumping out of an airplane if they don't have control over who packs their chute!) Economic, or shareholder, democracy is different than worker-owned cooperatives because the former assumes specialization in management and diversification of ownership, two important characteristics that are sacrificed with worker cooperatives.

Just as with political democracy, fully developed institutions are necessary to ensure economic democracy. Thus, a free market democratic capitalist model must develop institutional structures that insure stakeholders are empowered to exercise their interests through ownership and control, which means they must have the legal means to do so. We need laws that strengthen shareholder interests and ensure that their representatives on the board of directors are reliable agents independent of management.

Widespread ownership could help solve the agency problems inherent to organized labor. In the private sector, labor interests can obtain representation through ownership in conjunction with other stakeholders, such as shareholders and creditors. Organized union leadership could assist with coordinating stakeholders' interests, helping to solve collective action problems, while mitigating the short-term conflict between capital and labor interests. In effect, workers should become shareholders. This is a role that, to date, union organizations have eschewed. (We shall see how General Motors evolves with its large ownership position granted to the UAW.)

In the public sector we are witnessing a serious agency failure in labor organization and bargaining. Many state government budgets are being busted by wages, pensions, and healthcare benefits that have been promised to public employees under union contracts. Because the politicians who granted these benefits relied on public union dues for campaign donations, they had a strong incentive to comply with union demands. We can see the inherent conflict of interest here. The taxpayer is on the hook to pay off these liabilities, yet their agents—their elected politicians—abrogated their responsibilities to their constituents in order to get re-elected. The taxpayers had no real representation at the bargaining table when these labor contracts were negotiated. Unlike private unions, there is no real ownership stake available in the public goods sector, so it is likely these unions will eventually be regulated like public utilities, where contracts are determined by a political board accountable to voters. In this conflict, public unions have fixated on collective bargaining rights. But bargaining with *whom*? The taxpayer?

This brings us to the most pressing regulatory policy issue of our day— the principal-agent failures in financial markets. The financial industry is different from other sectors of the market because banks and shadow-banks are the only private institutions in the economy that have *the ability to create money through credit*. This privileged function means the financial sector has a significant impact on the macroeconomy through the very price of credit— the interest rate. Our model explains how interest rates are the most important signals that tell us how to balance our economic decisions over time. If these signals can be heavily distorted by the decisions of private agents, it becomes apparent that the incentives these agents face are a crucial policy issue. It is also why financial regulatory reform is such a contentious issue.

Most financial services are administered by agents acting for principals. This applies to bankers, investment bankers, fund managers, brokers, traders, etc. The potential for abuse is considerable because of the deliberate complexity and lack of transparency in financial transactions. Many books, some of them quite fair and balanced, have been written assigning blame for the recent financial crisis to various actors within the financial community, from mortgage lenders to commercial and investment bankers, to ratings agencies and dealers in financial derivatives.[64] The initial political reflex has been more laws, more regulation, more regulators, and more political oversight. Apparently, given the calamitous results, it is taken for granted that a self-regulating market was not enough.

Many critics of financial policy take aim at the conflict of interest between investment banking and commercial banking that was regulated by the Glass-Steagall Act from 1933, until it was repealed by the Financial Services Modernization Act of 1999. In essence, commercial banks receive deposits guaranteed by the federal government and make loans to business, while investment banks provide capital to business and also trade in a variety of speculative instruments. Mixing these two functions in the same firm, such as Citigroup, has led to conflicts of interest between the banks' customers and the banks' own speculative trading activities. In addition, risks undertaken in the banks' loan and proprietary trading portfolios were essentially underwritten by the insurance guarantees of the Federal Deposit Insurance Corporation and, ultimately, the Federal Reserve as lender of last resort to member banks. Glass-Steagall separated investment banks from commercial banks and the reason given for its repeal was that such regulation did not apply to foreign banking conglomerates. Thus, U.S. banking conglomerates were competitively disadvantaged in international capital markets, as foreign banks conducting both functions grew more profitable. Unfortunately, the outcome of combining commercial and investment banking led to excessive risk-taking that, when the crisis hit, threatened the solvency of the worldwide commercial banking industry. An obvious solution would be to reinstate Glass-Steagall regulation, but that is unlikely because the same anti-competitive results will recur.

The case for direct regulation with laws and monitoring can be overstated. The financial sector is already one of the most regulated industries in the world—Citigroup alone has over 100 regulators in the United States and over 400 worldwide, yet Citigroup was at the heart of the financial maelstrom. Increasing the number of regulatory agents is also costly and introduces greater potential for manipulation through regulatory capture.[65] Competition in financial markets is ruthlessly aggressive and innovative. Most egregious misconduct is controlled by this competition (it was not the Securities and Exchange Commission that uncovered the Bernie Madoff scandal, but a competing financial analyst). Given the questionable success of direct regulation, perhaps we should think outside the box by carefully considering the incentives financial agents face and how best to influence these incentives.

As a matter of policy, we should try to encourage financial innovation toward the goal of more prudent and effective risk management. This was the promise of securitization and financial derivatives that went awry. An obvious policy solution to control aberrant agent behavior in finance is greater transparency and rules of disclosure. But there is also a serious incentive problem that prevails in the financial industry that encourages agents to take outsized risks of the 'heads I win, tails you lose' variety. This incentive stems from the fact that financial risks are often taken on credit, or borrowed money—what the industry cynically calls OPM for Other People's Money.

The systemic risk arose when this perverse incentive received an added guarantee from the Federal Reserve. Fed policy under the Greenspan era was noted for massive injections of liquidity whenever a financial crisis threatened. It started with the stock market crash in 1987 and continued through the 1990s with the Mexican debt crisis of 1994, the Asian currency crisis of 1996, the Russian default of 1998, the Y2K scare, and the dotcom bust of 2000. Financial institutions and their traders learned all the wrong lessons from this liquidity policy they sardonically referred to as the "Greenspan put."[66]

It is likely we need some forms of reregulation and federal oversight on large commercial banks, but the wrong regulation can often be more costly than no regulation. The more effective cure may be the discipline of financial ruin. We should let banks and non-banks compete internationally, but only under a strict Federal Reserve policy stating that failed banks will be reorganized and restructured under federal bankruptcy laws. We need the discipline of bankruptcy and the consequence of losses to control moral hazard, while still allowing and encouraging financial innovation. This applies even more forcefully to the shadow banking system. This is the lesson we probably missed sending with the 2008 TARP bailouts and the backstop of quantitative easing.[67] Our financial reform efforts will spawn dangerous new moral hazards if we designate certain institutions as "too big to fail." As for exotic financial derivatives, establishing formal securities market exchanges that impose trading rules and regulations on these new untested, but widely marketed, financial instruments may be necessary.

However, the true problems of our financial sector harken back to a configuration of policies that favor financial interests through credit creation and debt leverage, allowing the tail of finance to wag the dog of the real economy. Between 1980 and 2000, financial industry profits rose from $32.4 billion to $195.8 billion and the industry's share of all U.S. profits went from 19% to 29%. By 2006 it was $427 billion and 32%. This is not to condemn finance unequivocally, as an open financial market operating according to objective rules is one of the most effective democratizing tools available in the world today. Finance has empowered developing country populations at an astounding rate, so the regulation of these markets has become a critical challenge. But financial and monetary policy has trumped sound economic principles and this is where our current problems lie. No financial system that operates under distorted incentive structures will find stability. Lending money was meant to be a slow, boring, incremental business. Unfortunately, changing technology and our own misguided and outdated policies have turned investment finance into the casino it is today. Only better-informed policies can turn it back.

CONCLUSION

One is hard-pressed to end this discussion, as it seems we have only scratched the surface of so many policy challenges. The format of this citizen-voter's guide to the economic complexity of our modern world aspires to provide a telescopic "big picture" perspective that offers more clarity than confusion. Hopefully, my exposition has convinced you that economics is a bit more understandable than you have been led to believe. This should not lead us to conclude that the controversies that plague economic science and the formulation of policy are easily settled, or that this guide provides any incontrovertible truth. Though beautiful, the world is a messy place, which is one of the things that makes it so fascinating. We should expect it to continue to be messy.

Let us conclude by summarizing nine basic lessons outlined in this guide:

1. Uncertainty is the defining characteristic of our changing world.
2. Loss aversion is the primary motivation determining human behavior.
3. Economic decisions revolve around inter-temporal consumption preferences, subject to the prior constraints of loss aversion.
4. The "interest rate" balances the future against the present.
5. All progress entails risk-taking; reward does not come without risk.
6. Managing the risk and rewards of change is the key political goal of a free, democratic society.

7. Our financial system is overly dependent on credit creation and debt.
8. Debt increases and concentrates risk.

9. Current macroeconomic models do not address distributional failures such as economic inequality.

We can separate these nine lessons into logical analytical categories, where the first six elucidate the basic laws of economics, irrespective of time or place. The next two pertain to specific financial policies enacted over the past century. The last lesson advocates a new direction for the future.

You might ask, after all this discussion, how exactly do we explain the financial crisis of 2008? Answering this question has not been the primary intent of this guide. Rather the attempt has been to impart the necessary knowledge and tools for the reader to develop the answer on his or her own. We have lots of villains: investment bankers and their traders, mortgage lenders, ratings agencies, government subsidies of the housing sector, government-sponsored enterprises like Fannie Mae and Freddie Mac, monetary authorities, politicians, home buyers everywhere; the list goes on. Some will regard this mess with disdain and say that it's all explained by human greed and selfishness. But this misses the point. Greed, or perhaps more accurately, self-interest, is an aspect of human nature. It is a constant in this regard and cannot fully explain any change in outcomes. Instead, we should identify the contextual factors that constrain greed, and promote ethical behavior and cooperation. The root cause of our financial crisis was the perversion of economic and financial incentives that all the above-mentioned actors faced, which started at the top with the decisions of the Federal Reserve. At heart, the crisis was a policy failure of calamitous proportions.

This guide has focused on the basic logic and practice of economic policy in order to understand this failure in all its dimensions. I have argued that the defining characteristic of our world is *uncertainty* and its associated *risks*. Uncertainty is the nature of a universe in flux and risk is our innate perception of how change prejudices our well-being and chances of survival. These two concepts shape our attempts to manage, through deliberate action, the unpredictability of the future.[68]

These actions include a variety of private and communal, or public, efforts. At the individual level, our desire to manage change has led to the evolution of private exchange markets whereby we seek gains, manage risks, and adapt to change. The creation of these private markets long predate established public economic institutions. Where private markets have failed, public institutions have attempted to fill the void. This public effort should be guided by the goal of managing the risks of change through the coordination and complementarity between private markets and public institutions. My public policy argument flows from these basic postulates.

Risks associated with uncertainty are managed through diversification, which can be realized through three complementary strategies: *self-insurance, private insurance pooling, and social insurance pooling*. Self-insurance requires the accumulation of real and financial assets and their diversification across asset classes. Private insurance requires *a competitive market* guided by accurate information, appropriate incentives, and accurate price signals—all of which minimize moral hazard and maximize the efficient provision of benefits. As a last resort, social insurance is inherently less efficient by design, but necessary where self-insurance and private insurance markets are incomplete. Examples of social risk management include unemployment insurance, disaster relief, and welfare transfers.

The three complementary strategies to manage risk require an institutional structure that ensures open and transparent competitive private markets. The requisites include appropriate rules, regulations, and practices that defend the rights of ownership and control over all real and financial assets. This is especially critical to the functioning of public corporations, the banking system, and the financial industry. To ensure our economic well-being, voters faced with various policy choices must understand the logic of private markets.

Many critics of democratic capitalism crusade against "free-market ideology." They claim that there are no "free markets" and that the abstraction is a chimera; a clever propaganda serving powerful private interests. These critics construct a straw man of "free market" purity only to disprove it with evidence of widespread market abuse. But this is a mere Sophist exercise. All markets are subject to rules of engagement in the marketplace. While purely free markets may be a theoretical abstraction, that fact does not diminish their heuristic or practical value. Theory is the lodestar that orients our practical policy decisions.

Free exchange markets are highly useful tools to create wealth, advance individual freedom, build trust, create social cohesion, and support pluralistic participatory democracy. They depend upon billions of human decisions interacting in a global "neural" network. As such, they are little more than amoral exchange networks that operate according to the freely expressed choices, or preferences, of these billions of decision makers. In this sense, markets are merely mechanisms for exercising *social choice*. This is just like democracy, which is a political exchange "market," where outcomes are determined by casting votes. Of course, these choices or preferences are not always socially optimal, and markets can, and do, fail. Economic markets can often reinforce the existing power relationships in a democratic society. But ultimately, markets are valued because *they provide feedback information* in the form of price and quantity signals. These signals guide us as we make judgments about optimality and, together with openness and transparency, even about what is morally just and what is not. Functioning competitive markets aid us in our goal of creating a better society, not only a materially superior one, but one that is also more just and fair.

Markets themselves are merely the means to an end. Some of us wish to get rich, some to be free of material worries, others wish to create a legacy, or to enjoy leisure and social enrichment. The ends we choose are as infinite as our numbers. From a social point of view, this becomes a philosophical and moral discussion about how one envisions the "good society." In the social sciences and humanities these are referred to as normative issues to differentiate them from positive arguments based on empirical evidence.

Another way of looking at the difference is that normative issues are framed as *what should be*, while positive issues are *what is*. Science deals with the real world, while philosophy ventures into the abstract.

The normative debate has not changed that much since the days of Socrates, Plato and Aristotle, though it is still worth engaging. But as a practical matter, the Founding Fathers did tackle these philosophical questions and codified their guidelines in the US Constitution. To reiterate, the Declaration of Independence tasked our government to guarantee its citizens' unalienable rights of *life, liberty and the pursuit of happiness*. This history argues that the primary objective of policy must be to ensure that people have freedom of choice and freedom of action to realize their individual preferences, subject to certain constraints of law and negative liberties.[69] Open, competitive markets are the most efficient mechanisms for achieving this objective. But markets are not free, efficient, or fair unless citizens are constantly vigilant. Human judgments are critical to maintaining the functioning markets that help us realize just and efficient outcomes.

Let us be clear on market intervention: the critical application of policy judgments is *not over final outcomes*, but over the *conditions or rules under which those outcomes obtain*. Sometimes a bad outcome is nothing more than bad luck. This is regrettable, but it's not a failure of the market. The policy issue regarding markets comes down to diminishing market distortions while enhancing market perfections.

A market distortion is one that impedes our freedom to pursue our economic goals, while a market perfection is one that enhances that quest.[70] I think we can agree that a stable and sustainable growing economy is an intermediate policy goal that enhances our individual preferences for personal freedom and economic security. We have examined some of the necessary conditions for a sustainable capitalist market economy. To obtain these conditions, we need an accurate understanding of economic behavior and the ways in which different incentives influence that behavior. Our model illustrates how we make economic decisions that determine our levels of consumption and saving, investment and production. For these decisions to be fluid and optimal, we need accurate prices, especially concerning the value of our money, or currency. We also need an accurate price for our time value of that money, which is the interest rate. These two prices are the most important from a policy standpoint. They are directly influenced in the short term by monetary policy through the banking system, and are determined in the long term by population demographics, technology, and competitive policies in the international economy.

Our fiscal policies should also be guided by the objectives of maximizing freedom of choice and freedom of action, while minimizing market distortions. Spending programs and tax policy should be geared to the goals of economic security and individual empowerment. I have made the argument that these goals are best achieved through enabling capital accumulation and broad equity participation in the production process. With the substitute of self-insurance that wealth provides, tax policy can help us achieve these objectives in ways that reduce the budget-busting provision of entitlements. If we accumulate adequate retirement or health savings funds, there is less dependence on Social Security and Medicare, which would make means-testing and the modernization of benefit calculations more politically palatable.

There are certain market failures inherent to capitalism that require policy remedies. The most critical of these are moral hazard, maldistributions of wealth and income, and principal-agent problems. Moral hazard is minimized through effective and appropriate insurance pooling. Principal-agent failures are mitigated by open competition, transparency, fiduciary laws, and credible sanctions for criminal violations. Bernie Madoff and Kenneth Lay are the poster boys for criminal behavior in this respect and there's not much more we can do except enforce sanctions that ensure crime does not pay, especially white collar crime. Corporate governance policy reforms should be focused on eliminating the conflict of interest between corporate management and the boards of directors. This may require new rules for corporate governance that seek to empower all stakeholders, especially labor, to exercise their interests over the ownership of the firm.

The Curse of the Market

This brings us to what I argue is the greatest policy challenge we face as a free society: the growing maldistribution of wealth and income, which ultimately determines the distribution of our resources. This is the dark side of a market mechanism that is both efficient and ruthlessly amoral when it comes to final outcomes. In certain aspects, inequality is a natural phenomenon. We all have different talents and innate skills that the market will reward disproportionately. Life is not fair and passing laws to redistribute wealth and income won't necessarily make it fairer. Our traditional market approach is to strive for equal opportunity and let the chips fall where they may. This leads economists and politicians to focus on education as the great equalizer. Equal access to education is tremendously important, but it is not enough.

The true source of income and wealth disparities is the ownership and control of financial capital. To understand this, one need only look at the following graphs of the growing disparity of incomes in the U.S. over time.

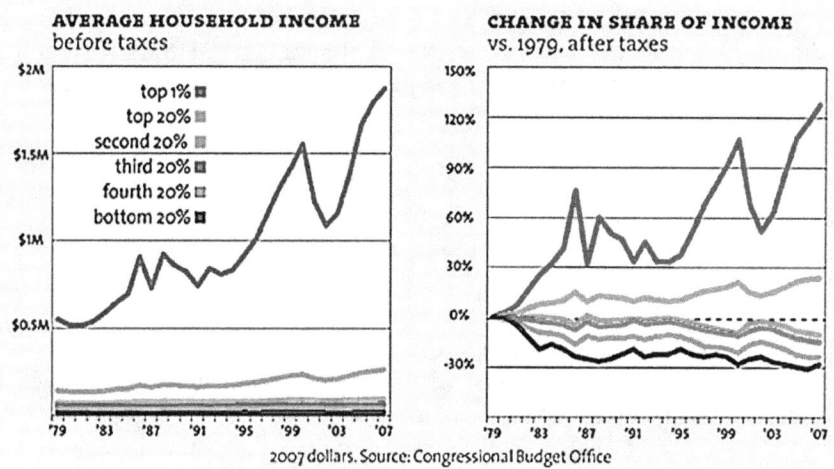

AVERAGE HOUSEHOLD INCOME
before taxes

CHANGE IN SHARE OF INCOME
vs. 1979, after taxes

2007 dollars. Source: Congressional Budget Office

We see here the changes in income from 1979-2007 separated out by income strata—quintiles from the top 20% to the bottom 20% contrasted against the top 1%. The maldistribution is obvious, with the most remarkable gains going to the top 1%. We should note the volatile swings in income for this group from year to year. There is no way these swings can logically be accounted for by education, changes in wages or salaries, or short-term income mobility. What is fueling these swings, and the widening income and wealth divide, is *the ownership of financial assets*. We can confirm this by tracing the periodic declines in top tier incomes to their direct causes: the financial market contractions in 1987, 1990-91 and 2000-01. We know that the crash of 2008 will display the same contraction of top tier incomes, and the same rebound immediately afterwards, due to the remedial policies that have been enacted since then. The policy "fixes" after each crash have only managed to restore and increase top-tier wealth.

We saw in our macroeconomic model that sustainable economic growth relies on a balance between consumption, savings, and investment over time. As a smaller group garners more and more of the resources of the economy, how will the funds be reallocated? Naturally, wealth is shifted from consumption to investment, as the rich can only consume so much. But excess investment with declining consumption demand means that investment will be channeled into less productive activities. We see this reflected in the "chase for yield" as markets reach new price highs and investment yields decline. The search for yield entails the assumption of larger risks with higher potential losses for miscalculation.

The timeworn correction for this situation is a market crash, when prices of risky investment assets plunge. This allows for prices to reset as unprofitable investments are liquidated and consumption demand contracts, putting downward pressure on all goods prices and incomes, affecting wages

101

and employment levels. After prices have bottomed out, resources become reallocated to more productive uses as determined by renewed consumption demand that is based on more realistic price levels. Like a phoenix, trade once again rises from the ashes.[71]

My key point is that the gap in incomes widens when financial markets boom and closes during financial crises. One might surmise that the cure for inequality is a good market crash, but we cannot solve the problem of inequality by equalizing poverty. (I hope that sounds like a bad idea, but it was tried by the former communist states of the USSR, China, and even Cuba.) The danger we face now is that Fed policy has attempted to short circuit the normal market adjustment process by reflating financial and real asset prices. This has been a deliberate goal of Chairman Bernanke and it can be seen in his attempts to prop up asset prices, from houses to bonds to equities, with low interest rates and quantitative easing. One wonders how prices will ever find their accurate levels under this continued distortion. The political and social costs of this policy are reflected in the growing disparities in income, wealth, and political influence as the incomes, wealth, and political influence of top 20% rise while the fortunes of the middle and lower income strata fall. This is no way to run a free market economy or a free society.

There is another interesting point to note in the interaction between financial markets and macroeconomic policy. We have noted several times that financial capital is valued according to the fundamental value of earnings cash flows magnified by the perception of confidence in the future trend of those earnings. In the stock market we can easily distinguish between the value assigned to real earnings and the value assigned to future expectations by comparing the fundamental value of the firm's earnings to the price/earnings multiple (called the P/E ratio). A P/E ratio of 10 means that investors are willing to pay $100 for $10 of annual earnings from an investment in a particular company. If investors are confident those earnings will go up, they may be willing to pay even more for those earnings in the short term, say $120 for $10 of present earnings yielding a P/E of 12 with the expectation that earnings will go up to $12 or more. Using these relationships as a rough gauge, we can see how much of the market valuation is being inflated by expectations and also determine whether those expectations reflect warranted confidence in the future. In the headiest days of the dot.com boom, many stocks had infinite P/E ratios because there were no earnings to speak of—all the valuations of these companies were in the eyes of the (be)holder.

Confidence is a matter of individual perception and one is free to gamble on hot air. However, if economic policy is inflating that confidence with easy credit and implicit guarantees—a serious violation of our macroeconomic policy model—then market instability will increase, as will the risks of crippling losses. Excess liquidity in the capital markets is often reflected in inflated stock prices that are not matched by real earnings growth. Mr. Bernanke seems to hope that higher asset values, which, as the basis of loan collateral, will shore up bank capital. Then, increased lending to business will fund productive investment and employment growth, causing business earnings to rise. But this puts the cart before the horse. Rising P/E ratios reflect growing confidence driven by real productivity gains. In other words, earnings rise, pushing up prices and P/E ratios. Rising prices do not pull up earnings. Confidence not confirmed by rising earnings and employment is not sustainable. We've already seen where that leads.

Excess leverage based on easy credit should be a central bank's nemesis. Regrettably, I believe our current policy direction not only increases systemic risks, but also is likely to lead to greater inequality, more asset bubbles and crashes, insufficient savings, high persistent unemployment, anemic growth, and declining opportunities for new entrants into the economy. If and when we run out of policy options, the consequences (such as a deep, persistent, crippling deflation) will be cruelly exacted by the market, largely hurting the poor and aggravating inequality. I believe it is up to us, as citizens and voters, to hold our government and politicians accountable and to steer the nation back toward a more stable and rational course.

Our politics does not exist in a theoretical vacuum. It too is subject to the forces of change, uncertainty, and loss aversion. American politics is conservative by design—the nature of the elective process reinforces loss aversion and the reticence to tackle problems proactively. This is why most of our policymaking is crisis driven, which explains why much of it is half-baked. As seasoned voters, we should all know by now that when a politician makes campaign promises to deliver a chicken in every pot and a Mercedes in every garage upon election, he, or she, is not to be believed.

We should be equally skeptical of promises on entitlements that avoid tough economic trade-offs. For the past century the preferred political solution to inequality in developed democracies has been tax and redistributionist policies, mostly through social insurance and welfare entitlement programs. These have been justified in terms of fairness, but are also conceived as a way to stimulate inadequate consumption demand during economic slowdowns. (When the economy slows down and unemployment increases, public expenditures on entitlement programs help take up the slack.) A concomitant to this 'social welfare state' has been a strong, organized, union labor movement. All of these rationales to address the problem of inequality are legitimate, but none are sufficient to insure a sustainable growing economy, nor a lasting solution to the inequality problem. Why?

Taxes intended to help redistribute income are targeted on income-producing activity, and thus changing the incentives that risk-takers face when making their investment decisions. The tax take raises the threshold level for investment and reduces the international competitiveness of U.S. business. Eventually, we get less and less tax revenues to redistribute and more jobs get outsourced. Unions have served several important functions in the past, but as the industrial economy transitions to an information and service economy, their functions have in many cases become obsolete or counter-productive to their members' goals. This is reflected in the decline of private union membership across all developed democracies, which has been offset by increased membership in public unions. Private unions are subject to the discipline of profits generated in the market, public unions are not. Public employee unions have only increased the deadweight costs of public sector spending, which depresses economic growth and distribution.

Some policy experts have advocated for a return to Roosevelt's New Deal from the 1940s. FDR's New Deal promised to provide public solutions to private problems with universal social insurance programs and the strong defense of organized labor. Because globalization and technology have created a different playing field for democratic capitalism, it may be time to rethink this model. A New "New Deal" modeled on this 'Old Deal' makes little sense going forward into the 21st century. If we all, as individuals, don't prudently spend, save, and invest over our lifetimes, there will be little to tax and redistribute through the public sector.

Some readers may conclude this guide is too ideologically biased in one form or another. A leftist, liberal perspective will see it as too pro-market and anti-government, while a rightist conservative one as too pliant on income and wealth inequalities. These criticisms appear contradictory based upon the simple dichotomy of the two these economic ideologies. The position I take is more complex and nuanced. I see the question of free markets vs. government regulation as one of looking at the glass as 90% full or 10% empty. [72] Market critics usually see the free market glass as 10% empty and desire more regulation. But the wrong regulation is often worse than no regulation.

Although this guide's ideological stance is pro-market—I would argue this is the only intellectually and empirically defensible position—it also recognizes the failures of orthodox macroeconomy theory to account for the ways financial markets misbehave and how this reality affects the macroeconomy. These failures are inherent to a misspecified macroeconomic orthodoxy (see Appendix B).[73] Managing the tensions between the two interpretations of free markets and market failures leaves adequate room for politics and a necessary role for government. But given that my position challenges both ends of the ideological spectrum, one shouldn't expect to find too many friends out in no-man's land. My aim has been, however, to overturn a few apple carts, rock a few boats, challenge conventional wisdom, incite controversy, and provoke more critical thinking.

To judge by the level of consensus reached in the profession, we can make a generalized short list of what economists know and don't know when it comes to the macroeconomy. First, what we do know:

1. Market competition works. Market liberalization has led to the unequaled creation of wealth around the world in the past century. This growth may be uneven and may foster societal externalities, such as inequality, pollution, and environmental degradation, but all societal problems are more easily managed by expanding the level of available resources.
2. Sustainable growth is the primary objective of economic policy. Long-term labor productivity and capital accumulation are the sources of real growth.
3. Open trade is a net gain to national economy, and globalization leverages the benefits of market liberalization and competition around the world.
4. Macro and micro economics have unresolved contradictions.

Here are the things we don't know, or can't agree upon:

1. How to use economic policy to ensure sustainable economic growth with the correct balance between consumption, savings, and investment over time.
2. How to analyze distributional processes that defy the standard modeling techniques of economic orthodoxy (see Appendix B); how to manage business cycles and maldistributions such as winner-take-all.
3. How to think outside the box with regard to:
   a. The design of policy to manage uncertainty.
   b. Policies to constrain crony capitalism and casino capitalism.

In this guide I have taken what we do know as a starting point and made some intuitive conjectures about how to proceed with what we don't know. The various ideas include:

1. Incorporating a more developed understanding of economic behavior under uncertainty and loss aversion as applied to policy analysis.
2. Greater incorporation of finance and capital markets into macroeconomic analysis.
3. Addressing the problem of income and wealth inequality as a distributional problem. This will require new modeling techniques to address the weaknesses of general equilibrium modeling (A discussion of promising new approaches goes far beyond this introductory guide, but the basic discussion is presented in Appendix B).

At the beginning of this book, in the Author's Note, I stated that, "The economy is the fine art of managing change through exchange." *Change* is what happens to us, and *exchange* is how we manage economic trade-offs in order to adapt to that change. The *change* and *exchange* to which we refer in economics is measured in terms of material well-being. In monetary terms it is reflected in incomes, profits, goods produced and consumed, prices, etc. There is a legitimate criticism that markets reinforce the configuration of power within a capitalist society. Success breeds success; the rich get richer while the poor subsist. But this criticism disregards the fact that when markets adhere to the principles of openness, transparency, and competition, they also break up concentrations of power. We may feel pessimistic and cynical about the inequalities of this world, the poverty and the injustice, the abuse of power and the fickleness of fortune, but I believe there is a more positive take-away from this discussion.

In a footnote to Chapter One, I alluded to the concept of *Time*. In a world of inequality, time is the great equalizer. Neither the rich nor poor know how much time they have and nothing can buy them more in the end. It is time, not money or material goods, that is the truly the scarcest resource in our lives. By the economic law of scarcity value, this makes time the most valuable economic resource we must manage. Though the rich man may be able to buy more free time with his money, global technological progress is helping us all leverage our own time in the same way. Consider how much money and resources it took to influence politics—to advertise, to promote through the mainstream media, to print and mail voter pamphlets. Now it is conceivable that it might only take a little time with a cost-free social network website. Technology is a great equalizer that raises the value of time relative to money and helps balance the inequalities of wealth and power with information and communication.

Time is what political and economic freedom can provide us. The true objective of a fine-tuned political economy is not a bigger GDP, but a society where we all have more freedom to enjoy this brief time of our lives. On this point I am as unequivocal as an economist can hope to be.

I'll close on a positive note with a quote from an article recently written by Walter Russell Mead titled, "The Future Still Belongs to America." [74]

> *The great trend of this century is the accelerating and deepening wave of change sweeping through every element of human life. Each year sees more scientists with better funding, better instruments and faster, smarter computers probing deeper and seeing further into the mysteries of the physical world. Each year more entrepreneurs are seeking to convert those discoveries and insights into ways to produce new things, or to make old things better and more cheaply. Each year the world's financial markets are more eager and better prepared to fund new startups, underwrite new investments, and otherwise help entrepreneurs and firms deploy new knowledge and insight more rapidly.*
>
> *Scientific and technological revolutions trigger economic, social and political upheavals. Industry migrates around the world at a breathtaking—and*

accelerating—rate. Hundreds of millions of people migrate to cities at an unprecedented pace. Each year the price of communication goes down and the means of communication increase.

New ideas disturb the peace of once-stable cultures. Young people grasp the possibilities of change and revolt at the conservatism of their elders. Sacred taboos and ancient hierarchies totter; women demand equality; citizens rise against monarchs. All over the world more tea is thrown into more harbors as more and more people decide that the times demand change.

This tsunami of change affects every society—and turbulent politics in so many countries make for a turbulent international environment. Managing, mastering and surviving change: These are the primary tasks of every ruler and polity. Increasingly these are also the primary tasks of every firm and household.

This challenge will not go away. On the contrary: It has increased, and it will go on increasing through the rest of our time. The 19th century was more tumultuous than its predecessor; the 20th was more tumultuous still, and the 21st will be the fastest, most exhilarating and most dangerous ride the world has ever seen.

Everybody is going to feel the stress, but the United States of America is better placed to surf this transformation than any other country. Change is our home field. It is who we are and what we do. Brazil may be the country of the future, but America is its hometown.

***

Dear Reader: If you have found this book useful, enjoyable, informative, or in need of improvement, please visit my Amazon Author web page on www.amazon.com/author/michaelharrington and leave a review. In the new world of eBooks and digital publishing, Amazon reviews are the best way to differentiate among books with recommendations or critiques helpful to readers such as yourself. Thank you for your valued input.

- Michael Harrington
  Los Angeles, CA
  May 2014

APPENDIX A

A Gross Over-Simplification of Economics

Consume now or later. These four words can help make sense of the macroeconomy, which is often presented with jargon-laden abstractions that non-economists find difficult to comprehend. In this brief appendix I will expound a bit on the logic of this statement and how it can be applied to real world events.

Most people understand consumption—we are a nation of shoppers— but most people don't stop to consider that everything we produce is ultimately consumed by someone or other. All resources and the production of goods and services are ultimately allocated toward one end: <u>*consumption*</u>. What we don't consume today we may save and/or invest for future consumption, perhaps by our descendants, but ultimately everything is consumed. After all, "You can't take it with you."

The real economy is generated by the millions of aggregate individual decisions on whether to consume now or later and the exchanges based on those decisions. The real economy can thus be represented by a simple conceptual relationship representing the trade-off between present consumption and future, or deferred, consumption. Symbolically we can represent the trade-off as:

$$\mathbf{C_{present}} \textit{ versus } \mathbf{C_{future}} \text{ or } \mathbf{C_p : C_f}$$

This basic conceptual formulation removes the distracting technical issues of savings, investment, interest rates, government spending, taxes, and currency values from the model. All these concepts can, nevertheless, be shown to flow from this initial framework. Savings and investment are inherently to this relationship because what we don't consume today we *save* for future consumption and/or *invest* in production in order to increase that future consumption. We can see then that the level of future consumption depends largely on what we do with our savings, or deferred consumption. If we gamble or frivol it away, future consumption will be less. We might prosaically call this trade-off our *inter-temporal consumption ratio* (ICR), which represents all our aggregate economic decisions over whether to consume now or later.

We can demonstrate the relationship to interest rates and economic growth if we take the formulation and express it as a divisor:

$$\frac{C_f}{C_p}$$

This is not a mathematical ratio like ½ or ¾, but a conceptual ratio of a constantly fluctuating relationship. As the ratio increases—in other words, as present consumption is deferred and saved and invested for future consumption—we can associate this with higher economic growth rates. As the ratio decreases, we can expect lower economic growth rates. If the interest rate goes up, we would expect higher savings rates and more present consumption deferred because of the investment opportunity. This should lead to higher growth rates. If savings rates are lowered, that leads to higher present consumption, less investment, and lower growth.

Imagine if the interest rate goes to zero. Would you be a lender? A zero rate means there is no compensation for *risk*, zero *time value of money,* and little to be gained from deferring the immediate gratification of present consumption. In the extreme, a zero interest rate implies a willful disregard, or disbelief, in the future. Naturally, when interest rates go to zero, or even negative numbers in real terms,[75] we expect the anomaly to be short-lived. We should question the Federal Reserve's Zero Interest Rate Policy, *aka* ZIRP. Their policy intent is to stimulate present consumption, but at what cost? How concerned about tomorrow are today's policymakers?

Let us consider another real world example. It is estimated that the savings rate in China is around 50% of income, so present consumption is very low and investment is quite high. The savings rate in the United States varies somewhere between 2-6%. Is it any wonder that China has been growing at double digit rates? Some analysts attribute China's higher savings rate to the lack of a social security safety net. Does this imply that the U.S. saves less and grows slower because of Social Security and Medicare? If we eliminate these programs, will we grow faster? Although this is an oversimplification, it does raise the right questions. It is more likely that China is growing so fast today because it simply did not grow for almost two generations. A lot of pent-up growth potential has been finally unleashed. We should also remember that every seller requires a buyer. Chinese exports depend heavily on foreign consumers. In terms of our model, we can see that China's high growth rates are not likely to persist unless domestic consumption demand (C_p) in China begins to expand, causing the savings rate to fall to a more reasonable level. Otherwise, the Chinese economy may run out of consumers for its vast production.

The ICR could be used as a tool of analysis to understand the effects of potential changes in the economy or in policy. First, each of us can ask how the change will affect our desires to avert losses; and second, how these desires will affect our decisions on consumption, saving, and investment over time. As we extrapolate the answers to millions of like-minded souls, the inter-temporal consumption ratio can help demonstrate how economic equilibrium and growth is maintained through a balanced consumption ratio:

- Too *much* present consumption means less saving and investment and a slower growth rate for future consumption.
- Too *little* present consumption leads to insufficient demand, less production and more unemployment in the present.
- Too *little* present consumption can also lead to excessive investment, which may lead to volatile asset bubbles and busts (in real estate, securities, art, gold, etc.).

Interest rates serve two purposes. First, they change the allocation between deferred and present consumption by increasing or decreasing the returns available to deferred consumption. Second, they balance present savings and investment, falling when savings supply exceeds investment and rising when investment demand exceeds the supply of savings. Equilibrium means savings equals investment. (Consumption and investment may also be borrowed from future time periods, but this is another unnecessary complication.)

This guide has argued for smooth adjustments between present and future consumption in order to create long-term sustainability. We can move into more sophisticated analysis by examining various factors that may cause changes to the equilibrium ICR. The two most important factors over the long run are demography and technological innovation.

1. Demography affects aggregate consumption due to the lifecycle pattern of consumption and saving, whereby we naturally consume more in our youth and old age and save more in our middle, or most productive, years (think Japan).
2. Technological innovation raises the expected rates of return for deferring consumption and investing our savings. This reflects the fact that we prefer present consumption unless we are compensated for putting it off and can expect even more in the future. The higher the expected returns, the more we will defer (think IT revolution).
3. The final factor affecting this ratio is the level of uncertainty that suffuses our economic decisions. Saving is a timeworn hedge against uncertainty. In times of volatility, saving increases while consumption and investment fall, irrespective of the interest rate. This explains the so-called savings trap where a decline in interest rates fails to

stimulate investment and consumption because of the overriding effect of uncertainty.

A final word on finance and price inflation/deflation. Financial markets are a complicated sideshow to the real economy and are important to the extent that they affect present and future consumption. The worldwide growth of finance has had a critical impact on the real economy, as witnessed with the 2008 financial crisis and its aftermath. Financial booms and busts lead to massive misallocations of capital and labor, reducing the economy's potential growth rate. While general price inflation/deflation does affect uncertainty, it does not appear directly in the consumption model because it is a monetary phenomenon that reflects changes in the nominal value of goods and services denominated in currency units.

Ideally, our simple model shows how the economy can achieve and maintain equilibrium between present and future consumption by constantly and smoothly adjusting to technological innovation and demographic change according to market price signals. Economic and social policy can enhance or impede this process.

APPENDIX B

What's Wrong with Economics?

It is a question worthy of a graduate seminar in economics, but we will try to illustrate the key issues in a few pages. One of the central assumptions in general equilibrium (GE) models that are widely used in neoclassical macroeconomics today is that people are pretty much alike, or homogeneous in their preferences. Consumers, workers, savers and investors, for example, all want to maximize utility and profits. A second assumption is that these preferences remain fairly fixed over time and do not vary or adapt under different circumstances. Lastly, economic models assume the availability of requisite information and the ability of individuals to process that information accurately.

Using these three basic assumptions, economic theory employs higher-order mathematics to build very complex and powerful models that enable us to study and understand the economic world we live in. Straight (or convex curve) functions usually yield clean solutions, known in economics as optimal equilibrium solutions. A good example is the graph of <u>supply and demand curves</u> that intersect at the equilibrium price. However, we have found that the assumptions cited above are frequently violated by real people acting in the real world, with significant implications for the results of the models. As argued in a recent book on the limitations of economic and financial models, the behavior of individuals determines value—and people *change their minds*.[76] The basic problem, according to the author, is that "in physics you're playing against God, and He doesn't change His laws very often. In finance, you're playing against God's creatures." And God's creatures use "their ephemeral opinions" to value assets. Moreover, most financial models "fail to reflect the complex reality of the world around them." The most serious weaknesses we have identified result from information failures and the ways in which we rationally adapt to these failures.

To conceptualize the difficulties of economic modeling, imagine a box of dried spaghetti pasta. Each strand of spaghetti represents an agent in our model. The individual strands can bend slightly without breaking, but they are mostly rigid and straight as an arrow. They cannot be folded back on themselves or twisted into a pretzel. Now, imagine building a model of a house or some other structure, such as a globe, with these sticks. The straight lines will intersect at many different points where you can glue them together. Depending on how big your model or how small the lengths of noodles, you can create a pretty good representation of curved surfaces using only straight lines. The model looks reasonably good, we can see what the model is meant to represent, and the structure holds together well.

Now, imagine trying to build the same model with wet, cooked spaghetti. Impossible. The strands wiggle around like worms, twisting and turning and refusing to retain a fixed shape. The model collapses into a tangled, gooey mess. This crude comparison illustrates the difference between an economic model that is built with simultaneous straight line equations that yield optimal solutions—those based on assumptions of homogeneous fixed preferences that don't change over time and that reflect perfect information—and the often sad reality of a messy world. Economic behavioralists have discovered that our preferences vary, they change over time as we receive feedback and our circumstances change, and often they are not fully informed because we lack the requisite information. People are not like dried spaghetti noodles, they are like cooked noodles – unpredictable. They are plagued by the uncertainty of their environment and are dominated by loss aversion. This creates serious limitations for modeling specific economic puzzles, especially those that relate to distributional dynamics characterized by variable preferences, feedback, and adaptability. Examples include inequality, the business cycle, networked market solutions, and information cascades. So, what are we to do?

First, let's not throw out the baby with the bathwater. Neo-classical GE models based on higher-order mathematics are very useful and powerful tools for explaining a wide range of market phenomena. Computer technology now offers us another powerful tool with simulation modeling. The exploding processing power of computers allows us to build market models from the bottom up using individual "agents" that can behave according to any number of simple rules that can be used in combination to create complexity. Individual agents can be unique in their preferences and adapt in an instant to changing circumstances, so our model doesn't need to be constrained by rigid, representative agents. We can simulate how these programmed agents interact, as in a market, and observe the results. In effect, we can build ourselves interactive economic worlds that mimic the real world and then observe how these models behave as we change parameters.

I believe these techniques will allow us to fill in the gaps of conventional economic theory and improve our understanding of market dynamics.[77] This promising new branch of economics is called agent-based computational economics. It's not as elegant or intimidating as general equilibrium models, but it can do things GE models cannot. It is a sign of progress that hopefully in fifty years we won't still be grappling with the same epistemological problems and policy failures.

APPENDIX C

THE CREDIT-DEBT MACHINE

The Credit-Debt flowchart graphic on the next page illustrates the "Credit-Debt Machine" that underpins the U.S. monetary system in its present configuration. Let us examine this in detail. As explained in the section in Chapter Two titled Financial Alchemy, the credit creation process starts with the Federal Reserve when it issues borrowing credits or provides liquid funds through open market purchases of bonds to the banking system (green arrow labeled Borrowing Credit$), buys toxic banking assets from banks (TARP), or purchases bonds directly from the Treasury (QE credit$). The banks and shadow banks then turn these credits into high-powered money through fractional reserve lending (Credit Multipliers) to businesses, consumers, and mortgage borrowers, and through margin loans to investors. The banks make money by receiving interest payments on these loans in excess of what they pay to the Federal Reserve. Banks and investors also buy Treasury bonds, providing credits to the government at the market interest rate.

The U.S. Treasury must fund Federal government expenditures (Gov. Spending and Entitlements), either through taxes or through borrowing (by selling Treasury notes and bonds to private investors, banks, the Fed and foreigners). The Treasury must pay back principal and interest on these obligations (all the red arrows coming out of the Treasury). The principal is constantly rolled over by selling new bonds at the prevailing interest rate. The government never has to pay back all its debt; it only has to service its borrowing needs (and we know it really doesn't even have to do that!). This is because the government has an infinite life, so it never needs to "settle up." However, if it needs to rollover an old bond at a low interest rate into a new bond at a higher interest rate, its payment liabilities will increase significantly.

We can see that this whole system relies primarily on the ability of taxpayers, which include businesses, consumers and homeowners, to continue to pay taxes to service a rising level of debt. It also relies on the willingness of foreigners to provide those credits by buying Treasury notes and bonds (Foreign credits). If the government borrows and spends to excess, this mechanism eventually must freeze up. The only policy option then will be to pay off all debts with money newly created by the Federal Reserve. Money creation risks hyper-inflation followed by a severe depression. Avoiding such dire consequences would entail a combination of fiscal austerity and monetary depreciation, which would translate into years of stagflation. *The true consequence of runaway debt is that it will depreciate the real value of everything we own, diminishing our standard of living.*

Obviously, the rational choice is to avoid excess borrowing and spending. Why is this so hard to achieve?

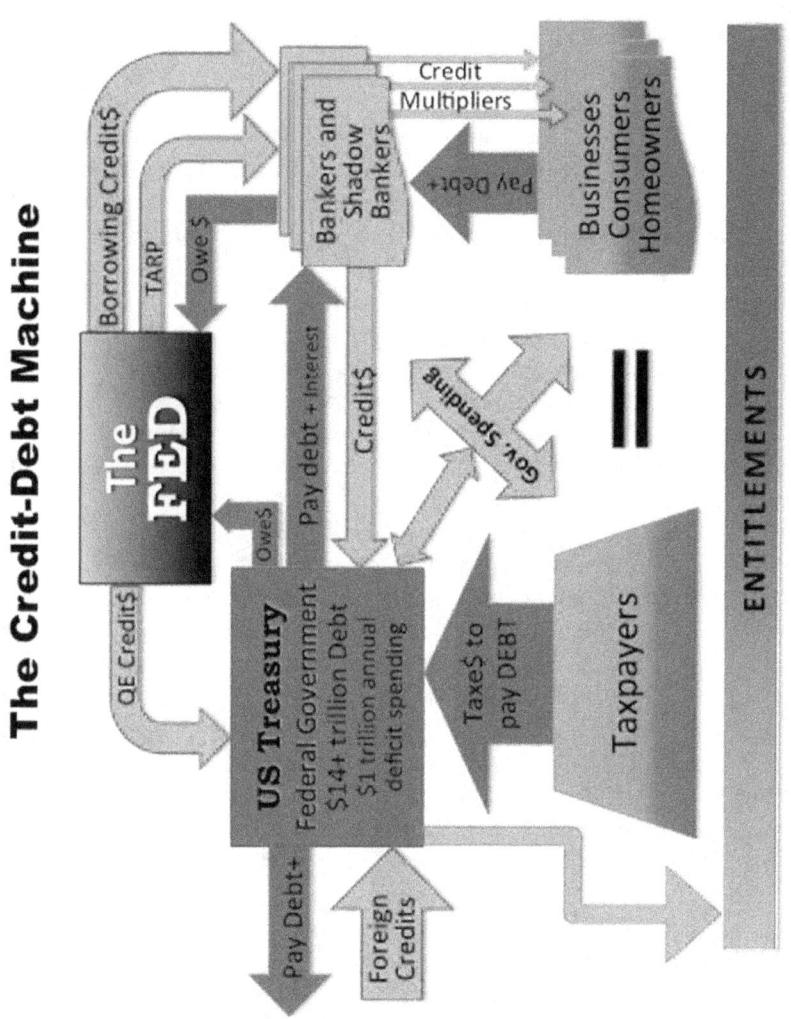

The Credit-Debt Machine

Source: Political Economy Simplified: A Citizen's Survival Guide

For the answer we need to consider the incentives of the major actors in the game. First, government spending is authorized by politicians who are eager to get re-elected by delivering public goods to their constituents. To ask politicians to cease and desist from formulating and funding government spending programs is like asking lions to stop eating gazelles – it's a form of political suicide.

Second, the banking and shadow banking industries feed at this same trough by providing the needed credit at a price. The more debt issued and credits provided to the government, the more the banks make in the difference between what they pay for credit and what they make in interest on loans or investments. In other words, they can borrow from the Fed at 0-1% and lend out to businesses, consumers, and homeowners at 5-18%. (Technically, this is like a form of modern seignorage – an arcane monetary concept that denotes the banking authority's ability to collect the difference between interest earned on securities acquired in exchange for bank notes and the costs of producing and distributing those notes.) The banking system's stake in credit creation and debt has enabled it to grow its profits from $32.4 billion to $427 billion in 25 years. These profits provide an enormous war chest for political lobbying and for placing financial industry alumni in government policymaking jobs. It's difficult to imagine anyone in a position of financial or political power desiring to reform this system.

Lastly, we can see that the people who pay the bills—the taxpaying businesses, consumers, workers and homeowners—have little political input into this process. We might then label this system a blatant case of 'taxation without representation.' As hard as it may be to change the debt-based monetary system, its current practice is unsustainable. The recent debt ceiling political crisis is evidence of the growing awareness of this fact among voters. Perhaps the best way to convey the gist of what has transpired is with a story. Let's call it the Washington Road Trip.

Imagine a car—a big fat gas-guzzling, over-powered U.S. luxury car or SUV—barreling down the highway. It's picking up speed under the driver's lead foot. The guys in front are in control, while those seated in back just came along for the ride. But now the car is careening recklessly and still picking up speed, giving them all second thoughts. One little guy is cowering against the door thinking about how *Thelma and Louise* ended.

The driver looks at the fuel gauge and says, "Hey, we need more gas. Somebody back there give me a credit card." (For the sake of the analogy, let's assume the car doesn't have to stop or slow down to refuel.)

Each of the poor folks in back says, "Not me. I'm tapped out. Over my limit. Can't even afford to pay down the balance I owe now."

The guys in front then focus on the little guy. "Hey, don't you have your rich uncle's credit card? Hand it over."

In a weak voice he replies, "Can't. He said if I used it again he would cut me off. Listen, can't we just put on the brakes and slow down a bit?"

At which point the guys in front start castigating and rebuking the little guy as a selfish, ignorant, lowly coward. Meanwhile the car is still picking up speed and the Grand Canyon looms dead ahead.

So, can we put some names to the actors in this tale? The driver is the chief executive and the guys in the front seat are the policymaking elites in the Senate, Fed, and Treasury. The joyriders in the back are the Congress and the little, fearful guy with a tight grip on his uncle's credit card is the Tea Party caucus. The guys too happy to pump the gas (at a price) are the bankers and financial industry. The sleeping Highway Patrolmen that just clocked the car's accelerating speed is Standard & Poor's and Moody's.

What we don't know yet is how the Washington Road Trip ends.

ABOUT THE AUTHOR

Michael Harrington has a broad background in the social sciences and the arts. He has earned advanced degrees in economics, finance, and political science and has worked in the securities and venture capital industries as an investment portfolio manager and financial analyst. In more recent years he has taught political science as a lecturer at the University of California and worked as an economics research fellow and public policy analyst. His research interests have encompassed macroeconomic policy, trade, social insurance, and international capital markets.

Harrington also harbors a life-long fascination with history, especially that of the Italian Renaissance. These enduring interests in social movements and artistic creativity during the Florentine Renaissance directed him toward the fascinating stories of Girolamo Savonarola, Niccolo Machiavelli, Lorenzo de' Medici, Michelangelo Buonarroti, and Leonardo da Vinci.

Other books by Michael Harrington:

The City of Man: A Trilogy
Inferno
Purgatorio
Paradiso

Saving Mona Lisa

In God We Trust

Trade and Social Insurance:
The Development of National Unemployment Insurance in
Advanced Industrial Democracies

These books can be found online at
www.amazon.com/author/michaelharrington

READING LIST

Books/films on the recent financial crisis:

Cassidy, John. *How Markets Fail.*

Fox, Justin. *The Myth of the Rational Market.*

Lewis, Michael. *The Big Short.*

Morgenson, Gretchen. *Reckless Endangerment.*

Ritholtz, Barry. *Bailout Nation*

Stiglitz, Joseph. *Freefall: America, Free Markets, and the Sinking of the World Economy.*

Tett, Julian. *Fool's Gold.*

Inside Job – Academy-Award winning documentary film.

Books investigating the study of economics, politics, and finance:

Derman, Emanuel. *Models. Behaving. Badly.*

Farmer, Roger. *How the Economy Works: Confidence, Crashes and Self-Fulfilling Prophecies*

Greider, William. Secrets of the Temple: *How the Federal Reserve Runs the Country*

Ip, Greg. *The Little Book of Economics*

Mandelbrot, Benoit. *The Misbehavior of Markets.*

Minsky, Hyman. *Stabilizing an Unstable Economy*

Paul, Ron. *End the Fed*

Rajan, Raghuram. *Fault Lines.*

Rajan, Raghuram and Luigi Zingales. *Saving Capitalism from the Capitalists*

Rickards, James. *Currency Wars: The Making of the Next Global Crisis*

Rothbard, Murray. *The Case Against the Fed*

Rothbard, Murray. *The Mystery of Banking*

Shiller, Robert. *Irrational Exuberance*

Shiller, Robert. *The New Financial Order: Risk in the 21st Century*

Shiller, Robert and George Akerlof. *Animal Spirits: How Human Psychology Drives the Economy, and Why It Matters for Global Capitalism*

Sowell, Thomas. *Basic Economics: A Common Sense Guide to the Economy*

Taleb, Nassim Nicholas. *Fooled By Randomness*.

Taleb, Nassim Nicholas. *The Black Swan: The Impact of the Highly Improbable.*

Warburton, Peter. *Debt and Delusion*

Weitzman, Martin. *The Share Economy*

Wheelan, Charles. *Naked Economics*

Classics:

Bernstein, Peter. *Against the Gods: The Remarkable Story of Risk.*

De Soto, Hernando. *The Other Path*

Friedman, Milton. *Capitalism and Freedom*

Friedman, Milton and Rose. *Free to Choose*

Galbraith, John Kenneth. *A Short History of Financial Euphoria*

Hayek, Friedrich. *The Road to Serfdom*

Hayek, Friedrich. *The Fatal Conceit*

Hazlitt, Henry. *Economics in One Lesson*

Kelso, Louis and Mortimer Adler. *The Capitalist Manifesto.*

GLOSSARY

Arbitrage

A trading strategy, when two assets are mispriced, to sell the higher priced asset and buy the lower priced asset, yielding a profit when the two prices converge.

Asset

Anything tangible or intangible that is capable of being owned or controlled to produce value and that is held to have positive economic value is considered an asset.

Bond

(No, not James Bond.) A debt security, in which the authorized issuer owes the holders a debt and, depending on the terms of the bond, is obliged to pay interest and/or to repay the principal at a later date, termed maturity. A bond is a formal contract to repay borrowed money with interest at fixed intervals.

Bretton Woods System

The international monetary regime established after World War II to manage the finance of international trade, currency exchange, and cross-border investment. The chief features of the Bretton Woods system were an obligation for each country to adopt a monetary policy that maintained the exchange rate by tying its currency to the U.S. dollar and the ability of the IMF to bridge temporary imbalances of payments.

Capital Asset

A factor of production, used to create goods or services in the production process. A capital asset is valued by the return it produces when employed. Since this return is an expected return in the future, capital value is often a function of expectations, infused either with confidence (positive value) or uncertainty (negative value).

Capital Asset Pricing Model (CAPM)

A formulaic model used to determine a theoretically appropriate required rate of return of an asset, if that asset is to be added to an already well-diversified portfolio, given that asset's non-diversifiable risk.

Capital Market

A market for securities (debt or equity), where business enterprises and governments can raise long-term funds.

Collateral

In lending agreements, collateral is a borrower's pledge of specific property to a lender, to secure repayment of a loan. The collateral serves as protection for a lender against a borrower's default - that is, any borrower failing to pay the principal and interest under the terms of a loan obligation.

Collective Action problem

A situation in which several individuals would all benefit from a certain action, which, however, has an associated cost making it implausible that anyone individually will undertake it. The rational choice is then to undertake this as a collective action the cost of which is shared.

Comparative Advantage

The law of comparative advantage shows that two countries (or other kinds of parties, such as individuals or firms) can both gain from trade if, in the absence of trade, they have *different* relative costs for producing the same goods. Even if one country is more efficient in the production of all goods, it can still gain by trading with a less-efficient country, as long as they have different *relative* efficiencies.

Consumption

That proportion of wealth or income that is consumed, as opposed to savings. Consumption is measured in different ways but mostly by the final purchase of goods and services by individuals.

Corporate governance

The set of processes, customs, policies, laws, and institutions affecting the way a corporation is directed, administered or controlled. Corporate governance also includes the relationships among the many stakeholders involved and the goals for which the corporation is governed.

Currency or Exchange Rate Regime

There are three basic categories of currency regimes: fixed, pegged, and floating. We currently operate under a floating rate regime, where currencies values are established by foreign exchange market trading. For a fixed regime see Gold Standard. For a pegged regime, see Bretton Woods.

Debt

Debt is a contractual obligation assumed by a borrower to repay the lender according to agreed-upon terms that usually include a regular payment of interest, plus the full principal of the loan to be paid-in-full at some future specified time.

Deflation

A decrease in the general price level of goods and services, occasioned by a decline in the availability of money and credit. Deflation is the opposite of inflation.

Demand

The desire to own anything, the ability to pay for it, and the willingness to pay (see also supply and demand). The term demand signifies the ability or the willingness to buy a particular commodity at a given point of time.

Derivatives, Financial

Financial instruments whose value depends on other, more basic, underlying variables. Such variables can be the price of another financial instrument (the underlying asset), interest rates, volatilities, indices, etc. Derivatives are used to manage risk through hedging.

Diversification

A means to reduce risk by investing in a variety of assets. If the asset values do not move up and down in perfect synchrony, a diversified portfolio will have less risk than the weighted average risk of its constituent assets, and often less risk than the least risky of its constituents.

Equilibrium

A state of the world where economic forces are balanced and in the absence of external influences the (equilibrium) values of economic variables will not change. It is the point, and price, at which quantity demanded and quantity supplied are equal.

Equity

Equity (or stock) represents the residual claim or ownership interest of the most junior class of investors in assets, after all liabilities and debts are paid. Stock shareholders bear more risk than bondholders because bondholders are paid first. When a company succeeds and the value of its stock rises, shareholders gain investment returns from dividends and capital gains.

Externalities

A cost or benefit, not transmitted through prices, incurred by a party who did not agree to the action causing the cost or benefit. A benefit in this case is called a positive externality or external benefit, while a cost is called a negative externality or external cost.

Factors of Production

Any commodities or services used to produce goods and services. 'Factors of production' may also refer specifically to the primary factors, which are land, labor, and capital goods applied to production.

Federal Reserve

The central banking system of the United States. It was created in 1913 with the enactment of the <u>Federal Reserve Act</u>, largely in response to a series of financial panics, particularly a severe panic in 1907. Over time, the roles and responsibilities of the Federal Reserve System have expanded and its structure has evolved. Its duties today, according to official Federal Reserve documentation, are to conduct the nation's monetary policy, supervise and regulate banking institutions, maintain the stability of the financial system and provide financial services to depository institutions, the U.S. government, and foreign official institutions.

Federal Reserve <u>Discount Rate</u>

The interest rate charged to banks for borrowing short-term funds directly from the Federal Reserve, also called the discount window.

<u>Federal Reserve Funds Rate</u>

The <u>interest rate</u> at which private depository institutions (mostly banks) lend balances (federal funds) at the Federal Reserve to other depository institutions, usually overnight. It is the interest rate banks charge each other for loans.

<u>Fiat Currency</u>

A fiat currency is a currency issued by the state and declared to be legal tender. It is not redeemable or convertible into any other commodity, such as gold or silver, and thus it holds no intrinsic value.

<u>Fiscal Policy</u>

Government economic policies that consist of expenditures and revenue collection through taxation.

<u>Foreign exchange market</u> (also forex, FX, or currency market)

The foreign exchange market is a worldwide decentralized financial market for the trading of currencies.

<u>Fractional-reserve banking</u>

Fractional reserve banking is best defined with a brief explanation. When a bank receives a $100 deposit it is required to hold a small reserve, roughly 10%, or $10 in our example, and then it is allowed to lend out the other 90%. This is repeated throughout the system, meaning the actual liquidity of the financial system is exponentially greater than the physical supply of the currency. This allows the money supply to be elastic in response to demand for capital, but at a cost. The Federal Reserve controls the reserve ratios for member banks, but unregulated, non-depositary banks such as investment banks were able to leverage up their credit instruments to as much as 40 to 1. A highly leveraged system is very sensitive to small changes in expectations, meaning the risk of real losses, or even a loss of confidence, is greatly increased. This is why we have bank runs.

General Equilibrium Theory (GE)

An economic theory that seeks to explain the behavior of supply, demand and prices in a whole economy with several or many markets, by seeking to prove that equilibrium prices for goods exist and that all prices are at equilibrium, hence *general* equilibrium.

Gold Standard

A monetary system in which the standard economic unit of account is a fixed weight of gold.

Inflation

A rise in the general price level of goods and services. Occasioned by an increase in the supply of money and credit.

Insurance

A form of risk management primarily used to diversify or hedge against the risk of a contingent, uncertain loss. Insurance is defined as the equitable transfer of the risk of a loss, from one entity to another, in exchange for payment.

Interest rate

The rate at which interest is paid by a borrower for the use of money that they borrow from a lender. There are many different interest rates that vary according to risk and liquidity. There are two basic components of the interest rate: the risk premium and the time premium. The first compensates the lender for the risk of loss is the loan is not repaid. The second compensates the lender for the time value of money.

Investment

The commitment of money or capital to the purchase of financial instruments or other assets so as to gain profitable returns in the form of interest, dividends, or appreciation of the value of the instrument (capital gains).

Labor

A measure of the work done by human beings. It is conventionally contrasted with other factors of production such as land and capital. The skill component of labor, such as that imparted by education or training, is often classified as human capital.

Liability

An obligation of an entity arising from past transactions or events, the settlement of which may result in the transfer or use of assets, provision of services or other yielding of economic benefits in the future.

Loss Aversion

People's tendency to strongly prefer avoiding losses to acquiring gains. Some studies suggest that losses are twice as powerful, psychologically, as gains. Loss aversion was first convincingly demonstrated by Amos Tversky and Daniel Kahneman, for which he won the Nobel Prize in economics.

Macroeconomics

The branch of economics dealing with the performance, structure, behavior, and decision-making of the entire economy.

Microeconomics

The branch of economics that studies the behavior of how the individual modern household and firms make decisions to allocate limited resources.

Modern Monetary Theory (MMT)

Not really a theory, MMT is an analytical framework for understanding monetary phenomena under a fiat currency regime, such as the U.S. dollar. In effect, MMT recognizes that the currency issuer (the Fed and U.S. Treasury/Federal government) can create money from credit at will and thus is unconstrained by sovereign debt burdens. A country like Greece, as part of the European Monetary Union, cannot issue its own currency; to fund deficits it must borrow from the international government debt market. Thus, Greece, like you or me, is a currency *user*, not issuer, and must pay its debts or go bankrupt. The U.S. government is not constrained by the need to pay off its debts. The more serious issue is whether the pay-offs will be worth anything in the future. That depends on the overall productivity of the U.S. economy.

Modern Portfolio Theory

A theory that demonstrates a risk diversification strategy where assets that fluctuate in price independently can be combined in a single investment portfolio to reduce overall risk.

Moral hazard

Moral hazard occurs when a party insulated from risk behaves differently than it would behave if it were fully exposed to the risk. This is an asymmetric informational problem that exists in all insurance pooling that is often controlled by behavior monitoring. Moral hazard also afflicts the principal-agent relationship.

Principal-Agent problem

The principal–agent problem or agency dilemma treats the difficulties that arise under conditions of incomplete and asymmetric information when a principal hires an agent, such as the problem of potential moral hazard and conflict of interest, in as much as the principal is hiring the agent to pursue the principal's interests.

Quantitative Easing

Quantitative easing (QE) is a central bank policy of directly buying bonds from the U.S. Treasury or government-backed mortgages, essentially injecting new funds into the financial system and providing a price floor under distressed financial assets. This is accomplished by the Fed purchasing U.S. Treasury debt with newly created credits. The Fed has also used these credits to buy toxic mortgage debt. By these methods, the central bank can provide funds at lower than zero interest rates in order to increase the monetary supply and combat deflationary forces. In essence, the Fed is monetizing the debt and increasing the money supply.

Rational Expectations Theory

A hypothesis in economics which states that agents' predictions of the future value of economically relevant variables are not systematically wrong in that all errors are random.

Risk

A state of uncertainty where some possible outcomes have an undesired effect or significant loss. Exposure to the possibility of loss, injury, or other adverse or unwelcome circumstance; a chance or situation involving such a possibility. Financial risk is defined by the variability of expected outcomes times the maximum loss exposure.

Risk-Adjusted Rate of Return

The rate of return on an investment asset that is adjusted for the level of risk. Finance theory shows by the security market line that there is one universal theoretical risk-adjusted rate of return to which all returns revert. This is like the odds ratios on the roulette table. This relationship between risk and return is represented mathematically by the Sharpe ratio.

Saving

Income not spent, also known as deferred consumption.

Security market line (SML)

The graphical representation of the Capital asset pricing model. It displays the expected rate of return of an individual security as a function of systematic, or non-diversifiable market risk.

Securitization

The financial practice of pooling various types of contractual debt such as residential mortgages, commercial mortgages, auto loans or credit card debt obligations and selling said debt as bonds, pass-through securities, or collateralized mortgage obligations to various investors. The strategy is to increase diversification of the 'portfolio' of assets and lower risk. Securitization assumes independence among the various assets that are securitized, a condition that broke down during the worldwide housing bubble.

Shadow Banking system

The shadow banking system consists of non-depository banks and other financial entities (e.g., investment banks, hedge funds, money market funds and insurers) that grew in size dramatically after the year 2000. These entities, not regulated like commercial banks, play an increasingly critical role in lending businesses the money necessary to operate. Also unlike commercial banks, they are able to speculate in financial markets.

Social Choice

Social choice is any process by which we make decisions in the collective. The process of voting is the most common case, but exchange markets are also social choice mechanisms where we "vote" with our demand and payment for certain goods and services.

Supply

The amount of product producers are willing and able to sell at a given price, all other factors being held constant (see also supply and demand).

Systemic Risk

In finance, systemic risk is the risk of collapse of an entire financial system or entire market, as opposed to risk associated with any one individual entity, group or component of a system.

Taxes

Does anyone really need a definition of taxes? However, there are various forms of taxation that affect economic behavior differently. There are taxes on production that are levied on capital and labor, as well as personal and business income. There are taxes on consumption, such as retail sales and value-added taxes. And there are wealth taxes levied on real property or inheritances. In general, the levy of a tax on an activity or entity tends to reduce that activity or lower the value of the entity.

Uncertainty

The lack of certainty. A state of having limited knowledge where it is impossible to exactly predict the probability of a future outcome.

Yield

In general, yield is the rate of return on an asset. Often used to compare debt securities like savings accounts and bonds. Because financial instruments fluctuate in value, yield is often different than the interest rate.

Yield Curve

The yield curve is the relation between the interest rate (or cost of borrowing) and the time to maturity of the debt for a given borrower. The time frame of the yield curve extends from overnight rates to 30 year bonds. The normal yield curve relates to the time value of money, where liquidity on a one-year loan differs significantly from a 30-year loan. The shape of the yield curve is a function of this liquidity preference, the supply and demand for credit, and the level of uncertainty in the economy.

NOTES

1 It took almost 200 years to accumulate the first $trillion of Federal government debt. Since 2007 we have added to it at over a $trillion per year. As of July 2011, it stands at $14.5 trillion. This is not as frightening as it sounds because, unlike you or me, governments never have to pay back debt and they can effectively create money to pay the interest (this is explained in the sections on money in Chapter Two). But the overall level and trend of national debt does have long-term consequences for our standard of living.

2 This credit-debt cycle is illustrated by a flow-chart graphic in Appendix C.

3 Daily foreign exchange (Forex) trading volume is now estimated at over $4 trillion *each day*.

4 See any articles by Daniel Kahneman and Amos Tversky. The development of their experimental findings is known as Prospect Theory.

5 The concept of time is fundamental to these five elements of our model. Time differentiates static (one-period) models from dynamic (two or more period) economic models. One should consider that the notion of time is what distinguishes humans from most other species. Time gives us a sense of our mortality and promotes the search for the meaning in our existence. Time also introduces change. Thus, time has a profound effect on our behavior. Static economic models are rather unrealistic in this light.

6 The chicken or the egg paradox results from a circular feedback process: you can't have eggs without a chicken and you can't get chickens without eggs. We'll find that the economy follows the same circular logic and economically we don't create "something from nothing."

7 Adam Smith identified the preeminence of consumption first in *The Wealth of Nations*: "Consumption is the sole end and purpose of all production; and the interest of the producer ought to be attended to only so far as it may be necessary for promoting that of the consumer."

8 Volatility in the agricultural sector—caused by droughts, floods and pestilence—goes with the uncertainty of weather. History is marked by such monumental events as the 19th century Irish potato famine and the 1930s dust bowl in the U.S. Midwest.

9 David Ricardo is famous for illustrating comparative advantage and the gains from trade, a concept that is fundamental part of every economics student's education. His simple examples can be referenced here: Comparative Advantage.

10 During a Senate hearing in March 2011, Federal Reserve Chairman Ben Bernanke was asked for his definition of the dollar. He replied, "Whatever

it will buy." Technically, his answer was wrong. Instead of defining the role of the dollar as a medium of exchange, a unit of account, and a store of value, Mr. Bernanke actually referred to what determined the 'value' of a dollar. The question was meant to focus on how the value of the dollar is affected by Federal Reserve monetary policy that helps determine the supply of dollars. The true *value* of the dollar is "whatever it will buy" divided by the supply of dollars in circulation.

[11] This relationship is represented by the famous <u>Quantity Theory of Money</u> that states as PQ = MV, where P = prices of goods, Q = quantity of goods, M = the money stock and V = the velocity, or turnover, of the money stock. So, P x Q equals the total value of goods and services and M x V equals the money supply. A stable currency value would imply that a constant ratio be maintained by PQ/MV. The quantity theory gets a bit too esoteric for our discussion of money, but the problem largely preoccupies our Federal Reserve. They have to anticipate how many new dollars (M) are needed based on the growth of PQ (another way of stating GDP) to keep the price level (dollar value) stable. Most economist liken this to trying to drive by looking in the rearview mirror.

[12] The <u>Federal Reserve System</u> was created in 1913 by Congress "…to provide for the establishment of Federal reserve banks, to furnish an elastic currency, to afford means of rediscounting commercial paper, to establish a more effective supervision of banking in the United States, and for other purposes." It should be noted that the Federal Reserve is *not* a Federal government agency, but a quasi-public/private institution. It is owned by its private member banks, but its policymaking committee, called the Federal Open Market Committee, is made up of twelve members, seven of which are appointed by the U.S. president and confirmed by the Senate.

[13] One important difference is that unlike we mortals, governments never die, so the government can carry a debt on its books in perpetuity as long as it can pay the interest on the debt. On the other hand, when we die our estates must settle our affairs. Another critical difference is that the government may control the supply of currency, meaning that it can pay back its debts by running the printing presses. Germany did this during the Weimar Republic, leading to the hyperinflation of the 1920s and the collapse of German society. Today, many countries are constrained because their governments must borrow in foreign currencies, which is why countries like Thailand, Argentina, and Iceland were forced into a debt crisis—they had to pay back in dollars or euros. So, printing money to pay debts is not as simple or painless as it sounds because governments eventually pay a high price for financial mismanagement. The U.S. remains a special case because of the dollar's status as a world reserve currency. More on this later.

---

[14] There are numerous interest rates in the financial system that apply to a wide range of borrowing needs. The interest rate that is controlled by the Fed is the most important one in policy terms. This is called the Fed Funds rate and it is the interbank rate that banks charge each other to borrow and lend banking reserves. All other interest rates in the financial system key off the Fed Funds rate.

[15] Increases in the price level (inflation) erode the real value of money (the functional currency) and other items with an underlying monetary nature (e.g. loans and bonds). Debtors who have debts with a fixed nominal rate of interest will see a reduction in the "real" interest rate as the inflation rate rises. The real interest on a loan is the nominal rate minus the inflation rate. For example, if you take a loan where the stated interest rate is 6% and the inflation rate is at 3%, the real interest rate that you are paying for the loan is 3%. It would also hold true that if you had a loan at a fixed interest rate of 6% and the inflation rate jumped to 20% you would have a real interest rate of -14%. Banks and other lenders adjust for this inflation risk either by including an inflation premium in the costs of lending the money by creating a higher initial stated interest rate or by setting the interest at a variable rate. As the rate of inflation decreases, this has the opposite (negative) effect on borrowers.

[16] China attempted the reverse logic—that a shrinking population could enhance economic growth—by enforcing its one child family policy. But a declining birth rate and shrinking population is a warning sign of future economic consequences. Most economic prognosticators now foresee a China that will grow old before it grows rich.

[17] This should grab your attention because economic theory assumes we are indifferent between gains and losses and always seek to maximize our gains. But this does not seem to be true. Think about your decisions and how the risk of loss affects them. Likewise, finance theory assumes people are risk averse, but this also is not always true. When faced with a likely loss, people are willing to take a risky gamble to avoid it. Also, in many situations people take on unnecessary risks in hopes of securing a large gain. These people are often found vacationing in Las Vegas or buying lottery tickets.

[18] See various articles by Daniel Kahneman and Amos Tversky.

[19] This price action is insured by <u>arbitrage trading</u>, which is just a fancy word for the decision to sell a high priced asset and buy a low priced asset with the expectation that the prices will converge. When we buy lower-priced, seasonal fruit we are conducting a form of arbitrage.

[20] The notion of the self-correcting economy has been at the heart of economic policy debates of the past century. Market fundamentalists believe the economy is largely self-correcting, provided there is no political

interference in the process. Interventionists believe government policy management is required to stabilize the economy. The problem is that politics will always intervene in the private economy, so the question becomes how, when, and how much. This conflict remains, and will remain, unresolved, at least for the foreseeable future.

[21] This is why we have <u>anti-trust</u> laws and <u>public utilities</u>. The reasons for these are not germane to our discussion but can easily be explained by the nature of certain industries.

[22] Despite being the named the Federal Reserve and the .gov web address, the system is not a part of, nor controlled by, the Federal government. Many claim this was a ploy to make the public think it was a Federal government agency. If so, it seems to have worked.

[23] While the Fed can force banks to redeem the credits it lent them (contract money), it cannot force them to make new loans by forcing them to borrow (create money). Thus, the process of Fed control over the money supply is often loosely described as pulling or pushing on a string. Pulling on a string works, but pushing on it doesn't work nearly as well. The Fed's ability to expand the money supply depends on the voluntary cooperation of the banks.

[24] It's important to remember that the US government is not bound by debt obligations the same way we mortals are. A government that issues it's own currency carries its liabilities forever, in other words, it never has to settle up, it can always issue more currency to pay debts. The danger then is not insolvency or bankruptcy, which is what you or I would face, but the gradual depreciation of the real assets and productive capacity of the dollar economy. A holder of US Treasury bonds (or for that matter, a Social Security claimant), will always be paid off, the question is whether that payment will be worth anything in real value terms.

[25] I say "can" because credit creation requires the cooperation of the banks to issue new loans and borrowers to borrow, neither of which is happening now with the de-leveraging response to the 2008 financial crisis.

[26] Goods prices were also held down by cheap foreign imports.

[27] Roger Farmer, *How The Economy Works*.

[28] Economists have often noted this, but in retrospect. Too little, too late. In the midst of the housing bubble, Federal Reserve Chairman Alan Greenspan said that asset bubbles were difficult to perceive until after they popped. The most notable analysis of financial crises is attributed to economist <u>Hyman Minsky</u>. An asset bubble driven by new credit is often referred to as a <u>Ponzi scheme</u>. A <u>Minsky moment</u> is that moment when the Ponzi scheme collapses, kind of like popping a balloon. In the words of one past Fed chairman, it is the Fed's job to take away the punch bowl just as the party begins to take off.

29 Statistically, uncertainty can be defined as the spread of the distribution of possibilities. This is called the variance of the distribution.

30 This means we don't let the market process alone determine the price, but assign this task to our so-called monetary experts who run the central bank. It is only pure faith that allows us to hope these experts are no less fallible than the pope!

31 A detailed discussion of these statistics is beyond the scope of this brief guide but can be referenced here: http://www.shadowstats.com/.

32 Over history international currency regimes have varied between fixed rates that do not change, pegged rates that are relatively fixed until the government unilaterally changes the rate (an example is when a nation fixes its currency to the value of the US$), and floating rates that vary day-today depending on currency trading. A discussion of these various regimes is unnecessary here except to note that the major trading states have been operating under a floating rate regime since 1971, when the U.S abrogated the Bretton Woods agreements.

33 The economist Frank Knight in his now famous book, *Risk, Uncertainty and Profit*, first formalized the difference between risk and uncertainty. Knight defined risk as a *measurable* quantity that depended either on a mathematical law of probability or an observed frequency distribution. Uncertainty is an *immeasurable* quantity because we lack data on which to base probability estimates. So taking a risk is like gambling in a casino, while uncertainty is like a meteor hitting New York City, getting eaten by a timber wolf in Central Park, or a nuclear terrorist attack. In Donald Rumsfeld's parlance risks would be "known unknowns," while uncertainties would be "unknown unknowns." Nature doesn't make a clear distinction—a threat is a threat—but our theories of economics and finance do, and often erroneously.

34 New financial instruments, such as derivatives, can be very efficient tools to diversify or hedge risk, *provided* they are transparent and regulated to prevent fraud.

35 This relationship between risk, return and price can be confusing. If the return of an investment stays the same, but the purchase price goes up, then the risk goes up (with higher price paid, there is more to lose) and the expected risk-adjusted rate of return falls. Remember the RAR is a ratio that will change as either risk or return changes.

36 To explore the fallacies of 'democratic' voting it is instructive to investigate Arrow's impossibility theorem.

37 Economist Robert Frank first examined the winner-take-all phenomenon in his 1995 book, *The Winner-Take-All Society*.

38 As a professional policy analyst and non-celebrity I must admit I find this a bit disconcerting.

³⁹ Two political scientists have also examined the political policies behind winner-take-all in their 2010 book, *Winner-Take-All Politics*.

⁴⁰ This follows the standard economic law of supply and demand: when supply increases and demand stays the same, the equilibrium price must fall in order to get supply and demand back into balance.

⁴¹ We should not confuse the *exchange value* of the dollar to its *real value*. Exchange value refers to the dollar's value relative to other currencies, such as the euro or yen. Real value refers to whatever the dollar can buy in terms of U.S. goods and services.

⁴² Inflation is different than relative price changes between different goods. For example, oil and gasoline prices can rise and other prices fall as we shift consumption patterns. Inflation is a rise in the general price level and must be accommodated by an increase in the supply of money. If the money supply does not increase, price pressures will lead to relative price changes. Heating oil and food prices may rise, while prices of discretionary goods like clothing or durable goods may fall.

⁴³ A nominal interest rate of 10% with an inflation rate of 12% yields a negative real rate of interest of -2%. Under these conditions a rational strategy is to borrow as much money as possible and buy hard assets that will hold their real value. This can go on only as long as lenders will lend at a negative return. In other words, not that long.

⁴⁴ For a good demonstration of rapid growth off a low base, we can take the experience of China and India over the past two decades. If one wants to have 10%+ growth rates all one has to do is to follow a generation or two of zero growth rates – there's no place to go but up.

⁴⁵ Fannie Mae = Federal National Mortgage Association (FNMA); Freddie Mac = Federal Home Loan Mortgage Corporation (FHLMC).

⁴⁶ Recapitalization of the real estate market means house prices rise as interest rates decline. For example, if you have an income of $50,000, you can afford a $150,000 home at 6.5% mortgage rates, but a $250,000 home at 4.5% rates. Lowering interest rates merely 'recapitalized' existing houses at a higher value – same house, higher value. It's illusory alchemy, though, because interest rates will go up again, forcing a recapitalization of the housing stock at lower price levels.

⁴⁷ Direct taxes are those you pay through federal, state and local levies. Indirect taxes occur with the depreciation of real assets through inflation and/or depreciation of the currency. These are often called "hidden" or "stealth" taxes. These are far more politically palatable because we don't "see" them.

⁴⁸ Some will argue here that there are three possible outcomes: hyper-inflation, deflation, or persistent stagflation, and that monetary policy can forestall both inflation and deflation. (See <u>MMT</u>) The rejoinder is that the

price of forestalling inflation and deflation is endless stagflation, as experienced for the past two decades in Japan. The resolution of this argument is realizing that monetary phenomena cannot substitute for real economic phenomena in the long term. Either we have productive policies that promote real wealth creation or we have a dangerous shell game of money illusion.

49 The last two decades in Japan help demonstrate what happens when prices don't reset to fundamental values. More recently we can contrast the policy responses of Iceland and Ireland to the 2008 banking crisis. Iceland let its banks fail and all domestic prices reset, Ireland bailed out its banks with new taxpayer debt, trying to maintain the banks solvency. Three years later, Iceland is recovering; Ireland is still in dire straits.

50 It's interesting to consider who this "Mr. Market" really is, since it seems very natural for us to want to personify this force of nature. Mr. Market is us, all of us together, behaving in different ways in order to survive, subject to the constraints of the physical world, the main constraint being scarce resources. We can see that this basic human impulse can never be defeated, as anti-market ideologues often suggest.

51 As opposed to cost-benefit analysis, I believe an expected risk-return assessment based on the overriding assumption of loss aversion might offer a more effective method to evaluate policy proposals.

52 First explained by economist Frédéric Bastiat in 1850 and recounted notably in Henry Hazlitt's classic book, *Economics in One Lesson.*

53 Whether public or private goods provision is more or less efficient should be an empirical question, not a rigid ideological position. In other words, we should test and study data that helps us compare the two and choose the best policies. Nevertheless, we should keep in mind that public and private goods are clearly defined and the burden of proof rests with the public sector as markets are the default position.

54 This simple philosophical principle was the inspiration for the title of Milton and Rose Friedman's classic work, *Free to Choose.*

55 Ideologues might object that this objective advocates prejudicial support for free market ideology, but this bias is less ideological than empirical and theoretical. Markets do for us what no bureaucracy or regulatory agency ever could by providing price-based market signals to all participants in the economy. This is a fairly uncontroversial view in economics, despite the financial meltdown and the failures of market finance.

56 A social insurance state is not socialism per se, but the socialization of risk does impose certain social constraints on individual freedom. One example is that we cannot opt out of Social Security or Medicare and stop paying the requisite taxes.

57 Social Security is a pay-as-you-go system that is guaranteed by the full faith

and credit of the U.S. government. In other words, the Federal government is compelled to tax current and future incomes sufficiently to meet its Social Security obligations. Unlike a private retirement or pension plan that accumulates and reinvests savings over time, Social Security transfers funds from productive workers to Social Security recipients.

58 You can observe in real time the accumulation of moral hazard costs and inadequate savings as they effect the budgetary items and liabilities of the U.S. government (i.e. the U.S. citizenry) at this website: http://www.usdebtclock.org/ Of course, the U.S. government can never go bankrupt and creates its own money for payment, so these liabilities will be paid in full. The question is whether these liabilities will maintain their real purchasing value.

59 The private insurance market often solves this problem with reinsurance. Interesting fact: reinsurance is the industry that made Warren Buffett rich.

60 Granted, this proposition is rather radical in that general equilibrium theory dismisses the possibility that prices in a market economy will not adjust to correct for such distortions and eventualities. Yet the mathematics of GE theory do not account for distributional dynamics, which is good reason to question its macroeconomic conclusions. I would argue that prices do correct in terms of unemployment and the sharp devaluation of capital assets. This would be the business cycle, which only begs the question of what will happen if Fed policy merely reinflates asset prices? Nevertheless, these propositions must be tested, but that requires different analytical tools and techniques. See agent-based computational economics.

61 Some may mistakenly believe "ownership" was the failed strategy of the George W. Bush administration, but this strategy offered little to speak of beyond inflated home ownership. The ownership we need is over the productive resources of the economy, which means more widespread equity ownership of the public corporation and a reversal of the privatization of U.S. companies.

62 TARP = Troubled Assets Relief Program.

63 This means any investment will have to secure higher returns to compensate for the risk plus pay the tax. Investments that fall short of this hurdle rate will not be undertaken or will result in losses.

64 If one is interested in assigning blame, I would recommend from the reading list, *Reckless Endangerment*, by Gretchen Morgenson.

65 Regulatory capture refers to the ability of the industry or company being regulated to "capture" the bureaucratic regulator to relax the regulation. This ability is the product of lobbying, where private interests entice regulators to their point of view on policy with various forms of payoffs, both legal and illegal. For the Masters of the Universe on Wall Street, enticing a low-paid civil servant to one's point of view has never been a

difficult prospect.

66 A <u>put option</u> is a financial derivative that establishes a floor for a security's price. A "Greenspan put" meant that if the market fell to a certain level, the Fed would enter the market and provide reserves to prevent further deterioration. Thus, there was limited downside and unlimited upside to every trade. We can imagine how this distorts prudent risk-taking behavior.

67 Quantitative easing (QE) is a central bank policy of directly buying bonds from the U.S. Treasury or government-backed mortgages, essentially injecting new funds into the financial system and providing a price floor under distressed financial assets.

68 I don't mean to suggest that risk precludes the more humanistic qualities of hope, altruism, and love. Rather it is the opposite, uncertainty is a necessary condition for us to hope. When faced with uncertainty and risk, loss is the downside, but hope is the upside.

69 In other words, we are not free to do whatever we want, only that which does not deprive someone else of their rights. So we must prevent cheating. The social goal is not to enable me to get rich by impoverishing you. Remember, "heads I win, tails you lose," is a natural and universal human instinct tempered only by a sense of moral justice and the enforcement of law.

70 This does not presume that political or social goals and individual economic goals always coincide, but social goals are achieved through democratic politics and democratic politics relies on a competitive political market.

71 Admittedly, this is overly simplistic but captures the basic outline of the business cycle. The crucial variable that has occupied macroeconomists is the downward inflexibility of wages and persistent unemployment leading to productive undercapacity.

72 In Capitalism and Freedom, Milton Friedman's wrote that "Fundamentally, there are only two ways to coordinating the economic activities of millions. One is central direction involving the use of coercion—the technique of the army and of the modern totalitarian state. The other is voluntary co-operation of individuals—the technique of the marketplace." I side with the freedom of the market.

73 I have summarized a critique of economic orthodoxy in the Appendix. The failures of all theories are found in the limitations or errors of their assumptions.

74 Walter Russell Mead, "The Future Still Belongs to America," *The Wall Street Journal,* July 2, 2011.

75 Interest rates are expressly in nominal terms but if inflation is present, the effective *real* rate may be negative. For example, if the interest rate is 3% and the inflation rate is 5%, then the real rate is -2%. In this case one should borrow to the max and use the funds to buy appreciating real